CRACKING CRIME

NIAMH O'CONNOR
Niamh O'Connor is Crime Correspondent for
Ireland on Sunday. She is also the author of
the No. 1 bestselling book on the Catherine
Nevin murder trial, *The Black Widow*.

Cracking Crime

JIM DONOVAN – FORENSIC DETECTIVE

NIAMH O'CONNOR

With a foreword by Professor John Harbison

THE O'BRIEN PRESS

DUBLIN

First published 2001 by The O'Brien Press Ltd,
20 Victoria Road, Dublin 6, Ireland.
Tel: +353 1 4923333; Fax: +353 1 4922777
E-mail: books@obrien.ie
Website: www.obrien.ie

ISBN: 0-86278-715-7

British Library Cataloguing-in-Publication Data
A catalogue record for this title is available from the
British Library

1 2 3 4 5 6 7 8 9 10
01 02 03 04 05 06 07

The O'Brien Press receives
assistance from

thearts
council
an chomhairle
ealaíon
50

Editing, typesetting, layout and design: The O'Brien Press Ltd
Colour separations: C&A Print Services Ltd
Printing: Cox & Wyman Ltd

PICTURE CREDITS

The author and publisher wish to thank the following for permission to reproduce photographs:
Picture section: p.1, Tom Burke, Independent Newspapers; p.3 (top), Eamonn Farrell,
Photocall Ireland; p.3 (bottom left), Paul Sharp, Photocall Ireland; p.3 (bottom right), John
Carthy; p.4 (top), Pacemaker Ltd; p.5 (bottom), Photocall Ireland; p.8 (top), Eamonn Farrell,
Photocall Ireland; p.8 (bottom left), The Star.

DEDICATION

This book is dedicated to Dr Donovan's wife and sisters; also to his colleagues in the Forensic Science Lab; medical personnel who helped over the years; the Garda Siochána, particularly the southern division of the Special Detective Unit; and to the staff at the Department of Justice with whom he has dealt.

ACKNOWLEDGEMENTS

Thanks to Brian, for everything; to family, friends, colleagues in *Ireland on Sunday* and to everyone who wanted to help explain and contribute to the remarkable life and career of Dr Donovan, from Professor John Harbison to the Dublin Fire Brigade. Thanks also go to my editors at The O'Brien Press: Rachel Pierce and Mary Webb. Above all, my profound thanks to Dr James Donovan himself for his unfailing kindness and cooperation.

AUTHOR'S NOTE

This book is not a biography. It is the remarkable story of the invaluable contribution of forensic science to the field of criminal investigation, and of the singular role which has been played by Dr James Donovan, Director of Ireland's Forensic Science Laboratory. It is based on a series of interviews with Dr Donovan and on case research. I decided to use the first-person narrative to retain the immediacy of the account related to me by Dr Donovan.

CONTENTS

FOREWORD

It is a privilege and an honour to contribute a foreword to a book about Dr Jim Donovan, the man who pioneered forensic science in Ireland. I use the term Ireland with reference to the jurisdiction of the Republic of Ireland, since the Northern Ireland Forensic Science Laboratory had been in operation for some time before that. When I commenced my duties as State Pathologist in October 1974, certain forensic scientific tasks were undertaken in the State Laboratory, then based on the top floor of the old College of Science in Upper Merrion Street, an area now shrouded in the trappings of power and occupied by the Taoiseach and his entourage. Given the limited facilities of the State Laboratory, the repertoire of tests carried out in there was very restricted, nevertheless Jim Donovan and his colleague, Ms Ann Conroy, undertook such tests as could be done to facilitate the Garda Síochána in their search for scientific evidence. Indeed, I can recall going up to the top floor with samples for tests, in search of Jim Donovan or his colleague, and wandering down a long narrow room or corridor with equipment on either side and bare floorboards. I wondered how they functioned there at all. This was before the State Laboratory was moved to the green pastures of Abbotstown, which in turn may be supplanted by the car park for a new National Stadium.

In those days, when bloodstains required identification – usually from a case of murder – a decision had to be made whether or not to send samples to the Forensic Science Laboratory of the Metropolitan Police in London. Jim Donovan, being a chemist, did not carry out biological tests and so a biological facility was not available to us in our own jurisdiction. Politics at the time seemed to rule out Belfast, just up the road.

Not long after this it was decided by 'The Establishment', whatever that was, to have our own forensic science laboratory. A competition was set up and I was asked to sit on an interview board which, happily, appointed Jim Donovan as our first forensic scientist. He was not strictly a director then since his only staff was one technician, the late Noel Trench. He was given a single room in the then Institute for Industrial Research and Standards in Glasnevin, just across the road from the Meteorological Office. That office, though it forecast the weather, did not forecast the blossoming of forensic science that began in the plain concrete building just across the road from it. This beginning would have been around 1975 or 1976. A little more of the Glasnevin premises later became available to the infant laboratory. However, around this time planning must have been going ahead for the Forensic Science Laboratory as we know it today as part of the overall technical services building for the Garda Síochána in the Phoenix Park. Certainly I recall interview boards for further scientists and was a member of at least one such panel. Scientists were appointed, with Jim as their first director, which post, happily, he still holds.

Direct dealings with Jim Donovan on a scientific basis lessened from then on because of the growth of the biological section, whose work dealt with the blood, semen and other biological problems that were more associated with murder than chemistry. Chemistry seemed to be more involved in cases of theft, road rage and subversion, with the various explosive traces and other chemical problems to which that gave rise. Hence visits to Jim in his laboratory – or by now his more palatial office – became more of a social nature than those of a practical consultation. Indeed his bright, top-floor office is a cause of some envy to me who, to this day, continue to work in an old garret in Trinity College! His work has even taken on an element of glamour; I refer to his attendance at European Committees of Standardisation in matters chemical. At least it must take him away from the more humdrum investigational matters that those of us who remain at home have continued to contend with.

Apart from his excellent brain and continued helpfulness in matters forensic whenever I call upon him, I must also refer to his fortitude. He has coped with the appalling injuries inflicted on him by Ireland's most infamous criminal: a bomb exploded under his own car. Despite the pain that this has caused him over the years, he has maintained a cheerfulness and warmth of character which is always a pleasure to enjoy when talking to him. I have admired how he manages to grapple with the administration of a very large laboratory – possibly the largest in this country – while at the same time carrying out his European duties concerning international crime and standardisation. His laboratory has achieved an international reputation and has hosted conferences which have attracted eminent scientists, not just within the British Isles, but from much further afield. The success of these meetings is attributable to his international reputation and to his warm personality, which we all know so well.

As a mere medical man I could not detail all the scientific advances that have grown and flourished under the guidance of Jim Donovan, but it is an impressive list. Chemistry, his own subject, has seen analytical investigation of fibres, of glass, of paint, of drugs and the plants from which they derive, of explosive residues and primers, within the realms of physics and chemistry. I am sure he has also kept an eye on the startling developments in the biological field, with particular reference to DNA technology. This has become so crucial, particularly in my own field of homicide investigation, in the identification of criminals from materials – however minute in their traces – that they leave behind on their victims.

Getting away from this encyclopaedic array of knowledge, I would like to try and touch on Jim's impish, at times even caustic sense of humour. Despite his problems and adversity, this comes through whenever he can be prevailed upon to tell a few stories of goings-on in either the international world or that of crime investigation. On the social side I recall with great pleasure attending an international forensic meeting in Tokyo and, believe it or not, even in that city, having pints of Guinness with him in an Irish pub. His contribution to the atmosphere of joviality in a very foreign shore was memorable.

To conclude these 'few words' about our Forensic Laboratory Director, Dr Jim Donovan, I can honestly say that he has been a steady friend and superb colleague no matter what crime investigative problem has cropped up over the last quarter century. It is therefore with great pleasure that I contribute this brief eulogy to a brave and brilliant man who has served his country supremely well and will, I hope, continue to do so. May his standard long fly high over the Phoenix Park.

Professor John Harbison
The State Pathologist
Department of Forensic Medicine

PROLOGUE: THE EXPLOSION

Wednesday, 6 January 1982

I SAW THE EXPLOSION BEFORE I HEARD IT. Had I been a mile from the flash-point, instead of just a few feet, it would have been exactly the same. Light waves travel faster than sound. That law of physics was first demonstrated by Sir Isaac Newton. In his case the experiment was based on observations of a cannon fired from a hill in the distance. I did not have the luxury of distance; the explosion was in my own car. One minute I was rounding a bend onto the Naas dual carriageway at Newlands Cross, the next I was enveloped by a dense, choking cloud of smoke with a soaring tongue of flame at its heart. Then came the ear-splitting explosion followed by the grind of wrenching metal as my car ruptured and spread – like pellets of lead discharged from a giant shotgun cartridge – leaving a gaping hole in the floor underneath my feet.

On that Wednesday morning, just before 8.30am, I was transformed. Where once I had been the crime detective, now I became the victim.

Forensically, I have always found human bodies to be particularly good at collecting flying debris. Later these pieces are invaluable when it comes to reconstructing a crime. My own body was no different. A year on, surgeons were still removing metal fragments of the fawn-coloured Fiat 131 from inside my abdomen. Around the same time, a piece of iron fell out of the sole of my foot – of its own volition.

But immediately after the device detonated, my thoughts were concentrated solely on getting out of the wreckage. I remember wondering why I couldn't remove my right hand from the steering wheel. I could see my fingers locked around it but not the lacerations to my wrist. It was winter and I was wearing gloves. I didn't know it then, but my ulnar and median nerves at the right wrist had been shattered, preventing messages being routed from the brain to the hand.

I could not move my legs. With my left hand I reached down and found my lower leg turned from flesh and bone to pulp. Afterwards my surgeons informed me that many of the long-term injuries to my lower legs were attributable to this point in time when my brain shut off the blood-flow to avert a sudden, catastrophic drop in blood pressure. My life was saved but no message could ever again be relayed back from my legs to say 'everything's okay'. Consequently, my circulation has never restored itself and my wounds have been unable to ever fully heal. The damage has therefore been prolonged.

But back then, for those few minutes, time was stalled in the present. Perhaps that is what is meant by the phrase 'my life flashed before my eyes'. There was time, for instance, to ask myself a million times over, why I had not been more careful. There had been two attempts on my life already, the last one less than a month previously and in almost exactly this same spot.

There was time too to realise that the three youths sneering at me from the yellow mini immediately before the blast were somehow involved. But the most puzzling of all the lightning flow of images demanding to be processed was that of pieces of my foot flying up before my eyes – I could not make sense of this at all. All these thoughts were swallowed by unconsciousness as my sight began to dim.

* * *

Why was I blown up? Who were my enemies? What threat did I pose to them? The answer lies in my chosen profession – forensic scientist.

All crimes leave evidence, and it is the job of the forensic scientist to link that evidence to the criminal in such a way that it proves his or her guilt in a court of law beyond a reasonable doubt. An American judge defined the importance of decoding crime-scene evidence when he said of every criminal:

> Wherever he steps, whatever he touches, whatever he leaves, even unconsciously will serve as silent evidence against him. Not only his fingerprints or his footprints, but his hair, the fibres from his clothing, the glass he breaks, the tool-mark he leaves, the paint he scratches, the blood or semen that he deposits or collects – all these bear mute witness against him. This is evidence that does not forget … Physical evidence cannot be wrong; it cannot perjure itself; it cannot be wholly absent. Only its interpretation can err. Only human failure to find it, study and understand it, can diminish its value.

But sometimes the truth is unpalatable, particularly to those whom it condemns or exposes. And while the forensic scientist's only weapon is the microscope, his adversaries have a much larger and more deadly arsenal at their disposal.

And they are not afraid to use it.

The bomb placed under my car was proof that Dublin's most notorious criminal would stop at nothing to prevent the development of forensic science in Ireland. That man was Martin Cahill.

PART ONE
THE DUEL
FORENSICS vs MARTIN CAHILL

CHAPTER 1:
THROWING DOWN THE GAUNTLET

The Murder of John Copeland

March 1975: ALTHOUGH I DID NOT KNOW IT THEN, the very first murder case in which I ever gave evidence was to lead irrevocably to the day that changed my life. And, of course, it involved a Cahill.

Twenty-four-year-old John Copeland lived in a ground-floor flat in Palmerston Road, Rathmines, with his wife, Colette. They had been married for only two months and John had just started a new job in the Central Bank. The couple were looking forward to buying a house and beginning a family. Life was good. On the night of 24 March 1975 John Copeland returned home to find a burglar in his flat. A physically strong young man, weighing fifteen stone, and a keen rugby player, John did not hesitate to tackle the intruder. The pair struggled, smashing a flowerpot in the fracas. The burglar grabbed a breadknife from a drawer in the kitchenette and stabbed John Copeland through the heart. The assailant then withdrew the knife and ran from the flat. Although fatally wounded, John followed him out of the house and into the garden before collapsing at the front gate. John Copeland died shortly after admission to St Vincent's Hospital.

Gardaí recovered a bloodstained knife from the scene of the crime. It measured fourteen inches and had been embedded two inches deep into the ground in the garden of the flat. The knife had a serrated edge and a blunt tip. At the trial it was stated that it had required significant force to drive this knife through the heart and lungs of the victim.

Three hours after the attack, gardaí went to Hollyfield Buildings, a dilapidated tenement in Rathmines, not far from John Copeland's flat. Hollyfield was home to Martin Cahill and his brothers, already well known to the gardaí for a range of criminal activities. At this time the Cahills had a reputation for burglary, specialising in the trade of colour TVs, and the crime had all the elements of a botched burglary.

John Copeland was everything the Cahills were not. Born in Huntington, near Gorey, he came from a religious, farming background, and was head boy in his final year at Kilkenny College. He went on to study at University College Dublin from where he graduated with a degree in Agricultural Economics, obtaining first class honours. He was later awarded a Master of Arts degree. He was a member of Old Wesley Rugby club.

Into this world entered Anthony and Michael Cahill – younger brothers of Martin – who had been in and out of reform schools and prisons all their blighted lives. The lives of the Cahills and the Copelands should never have collided: Anthony and Michael had made good their escape on a scooter after robbing the Copelands's flat and John Copeland should not have encountered the burglars at all. But one of those inexplicable twists of fate intervened and determined their paths would cross. Anthony discovered that he had forgotten his torch and decided to return to the scene to collect it – alone. By now John Copeland was on his way home after rugby practice.

Gardaí questioned both Michael and Anthony Cahill. A slip of the tongue gave them the break they needed. During his interrogation, Michael landed his brother in trouble by blurting out that he himself had nothing to do with Copeland's murder: 'It was Anthony,' he said. When it was put to him, Anthony denied the murder but the police were convinced that he was lying. They collected items of the Cahill brothers' clothing and brought them back to me to try and find any evidence linking them to the flat on the night of the murder.

Forensically there was plenty of material to go on. But the case was doubly important to me. It was my first murder case and I needed to show my superiors the potential of forensic science in fighting crime in order to convince them to invest in this new tool at their disposal.

On 25 March 1975 I began documenting the evidence from the scene of the murder in Rathmines. It included a pair of black boots, a small sample of glass from the carpet of the murdered man's livingroom, a sample of glass from the broken window of the door and samples of a broken flowerpot taken from the scene of the crime. Later I received a pair of brown leather-soled shoes belonging to the victim, black boots belonging to Anthony Cahill and samples of the contents of the broken flowerpot, taken from the carpet at 79 Palmerston Road. I was also given a rubber mat from Anthony Cahill's motor scooter, the blue round-necked pullover with yellow and grey stripes that Cahill wore on the night of the attack and a small torch he had been carrying. I went to the Copeland's flat myself and took a sample of carpet fluff, which was not as insignificant as it may sound.

In the soles of Anthony's boots I found fragments of glass, redbrick-type material, fibres, hairs and chips of marble-type stone. The glass fragments were the same as that which the intruders had broken when smashing the glass of the door to gain access to the flat. They also matched the type of glass taken from the broken window and on the carpet. The amount of glass still clinging to the soles indicated that the wearer had walked over broken glass a short time before gardaí recovered them. Normal wear will cause an article to shed foreign matter which has adhered to it at a high rate; after four hours less than eighteen percent of the material will remain.

All in all, the chances of the glass on the boots having come from the door were about one hundred to one. The odds of them not coming from the same source were about 200 to one.

I also found the same type of glass particles – matching in composition and refractive index (the way they reflect light) – as that found in the grit taken from the rubber mat of Anthony Cahill's motor scooter and the same as a fragment embedded in the base of the small black torch.

The sample of fluff I took from the carpet of the Copelands's livingroom floor consisted of rayon fibres whose colours, diameter and length matched those found on the soles of Anthony Cahill's black boots. It was exactly as I had suspected when I went to the flat in the first place.

I also found a small bundle of white silk fibres on the right heel of the black boots, and the same white silk fibres, of the same length, on the left sole of the shoes of John Copeland. Although white silk fibres are common, the probability of them being present on both Cahill's boots and John Copeland's shoes would have been extremely coincidental. Working out the likelihood of this being a coincidence would require finding out how much white silk was being worn and therefore shed on carpets throughout the country!

There was also a piece of red wool fibre, one centimetre in length, on the left sole of Cahill's boots, another on the pullover Cahill had been wearing, and another on the sole of the shoe of the victim. After contacting all the wool manufacturers and distributors, we discovered that this particular type of yarn was withdrawn from sale in June 1971, having been introduced on the market in mid-1967. It had been popular while on the market but represented only a small percentage of all knitting yarns. It turned out that Colette Copeland was an avid knitter and had been knitting a jersey for her husband from this same red wool.

In the broken flowerpot taken from the floor of the flat, I found two dog hairs and there were also dog hairs on the rubber mat of Anthony Cahill's motor scooter. These were 3cm to 4cm long and grey. It was not possible then to determine from the hairs what species of dog they belonged to, although nowadays it could be done by DNA testing, if the root of the hair were attached.

I analysed the composition of the flowerpot itself because I suspected that it was the source of three pink-coloured smear marks on the left heel of Cahill's black boot. Sure enough, the pot was an old-fashioned clay type, and by pressing a piece of the pot, I was able to make a pink smear similar to the stain. An examination of the stain showed it to be made of the same materials as the flowerpot.

Embedded in the sole of Cahill's boot were twenty-three marble chips of calcium silicate. There were seven more chips in the grit from the rubber mat of his scooter and one in the shoe of John Copeland. It seemed reasonable to deduce that these stone chips might have been a finish on the top of the flowerpot or used to improve the drainage within the clay of the pot and had scattered when the pot was smashed during the struggle. They are fairly uncommon.

There were no prints on the murder weapon but, in all, seven items were found which were common to Cahill's black boots and the floor of the flat and the shoes of John Copeland: glass, fluff (rayon in carpet), silk fibres, acrylic fibres, wool, dog hair and marble chips.

The odds against the glass on the boots not coming from the flat were twenty to one against. The odds of Cahill picking up from somewhere else exactly the same type of glass and flower-pot fragments as were in the flat were 2,000 to one. And the odds of over seven other items being linked to Cahill and the flat were high enough to demonstrate a definite connection.

At the first murder trial of Anthony Cahill, in December 1976, the jury voted eleven to one in favour of conviction, but a unanimous verdict was necessary and a re-trial was ordered.

At the new trial in the Central Criminal Court in December 1977 Anthony Cahill pleaded 'Not Guilty' to the murder of John Copeland. He had admitted that he was involved in housebreaking in the Rathmines and Rathgar area, but denied breaking into John Copeland's flat. His defence put forward the suggestion that the dead man might have fallen on the knife in the course of the struggle – a proposition described by State Pathologist Dr John Harbison as 'a little far fetched'.

On 20 December the jury retired to consider their verdict. They returned after two hours. Despite the weight of forensic evidence against him, Anthony Cahill was found not guilty of the murder of John Copeland.

* * *

My findings in this case got the attention of my superiors. Unfortunately, they also made an impression on someone else – Martin Cahill. I believe that he, more than any other criminal at the time, could see the potentially devastating implications of this new science for his chosen career. It was probably the point at which Martin Cahill began to consider forensic science as his first real adversary, and took umbrage with me. Certainly he learned from what had happened in this case; he began instructing his cronies to wear socks over their shoes and to shed them and an outer layer of clothing after doing a 'job'.

However, the Cahills continued to carry out crime, and I continued to analyse the traces left behind. For a while it seemed that Martin accepted that he could not beat science. On 24 November 1977 he was sentenced to four years for receiving a stolen car which he had planned to use in an armed robbery. He pleaded guilty after I found two of his hairs in a balaclava taken from the car. While he was in prison he had plenty of time to think about revenge.

The Kidnapping of Ambrose Sheridan

10 DECEMBER 1978: MARTIN CAHILL WAS IN MOUNTJOY, and in his absence his brothers were getting more careless; they ignored his warnings about evidence. Another Cahill brother, Eddie, and a career criminal, Harry Melia, attempted to kidnap the manager of the Belgard Inn from his home at Belgard Heights in Tallaght. It was a Sunday evening when the pair approached the house, armed with iron bars. Eddie moved to the side of the house, jemmied open the fuse-box and cut the mains. He was not wearing gloves.

As the lights in the house went out, the owner, Ambrose Sheridan, opened the hall door to see if the neighbours had also been hit by a power cut. The pair sprung inside, attacking him with an iron bar. His wife, Eileen, was in the lounge and started screaming. She was beaten savagely for her resistance and forced upstairs to a bedroom, where it was planned that she would be held hostage to make her husband comply. Both she and her husband put up a vigorous struggle; the hall was soaked with bloodstains. Eddie Cahill attempted to drag Mr Sheridan out of the house and take him to the pub to hand over the weekend takings. But despite a serious assault, and having been dragged through fields in Cookstown Industrial Estate, Sheridan managed to escape. The plan was aborted and Cahill and Melia were fleeing the scene in a Granada GLX when gardaí suddenly appeared in the car behind. As his brother Anthony's recent prosecution had hinged on forensics, Eddie had been schooled to get rid of all evidence and he threw out of the car a black pinstripe jacket that was covered in Sheridan's blood.

Gardaí saw the jacket flung from the window and knew that

they were on to something. After a high-speed chase they picked the pair up. Three days later I had a pair of Eddie Cahill's brown boots in front of me. It was clear that he had done his best to polish them clean, but not clean enough. Mud remained in the vault of the left sole, which had also caught some fibres.

I found that the mud and grass on the boots were the same as a sample taken from Eddie's bedroom, reducing the probability that anyone other than he had worn them. The grass on the boots and in the bedroom was found to be the same as that from a field between the Sheridans's house and Cookstown Estate. There were mustard-coloured polyester fibres on the soles of the brown boots that matched the Sheridans's mustard carpet in the lounge of Belgard Heights. Pale pink acrylic fibres on the soles of Eddie's boots were the same colour and composition as the fibres of the pink carpet from the bedroom. The blood on the pinstripe jacket thrown from the getaway car belonged to the same blood group as Ambrose Sheridan's and matched blood found on his shirt.

As a result of this evidence, another Cahill brother was sent down.

Robbery of Smurfit Paper Mills

JULY 1978: WHEN ANTHONY CAHILL CAME OUT OF PRISON after serving a sentence for the burglary of John Copeland's flat, he went straight back to his old habits. With his elder brother, John, he hit the Smurfit Paper Mills in Clonskeagh for the payroll. But the gardaí were on the scene before they could get away, and in the shoot-out that ensued, John was shot. The robbers abandoned their motorbike on Raglan Road in Ballsbridge and tried to escape by jumping through the window of a flat, in the process supplying me with a host of new contact evidence. As gardaí arrested the pair, John tried to dig the bullet out of his chest with his hands.

On John Cahill's black jacket I found lead, copper and barium, consistent with him having discharged a firearm, or coming into contact with it. On his shoes there was white dust that was the same composition as dust from Smurfit's hall.

I found lead, copper and barium on the denim trousers of Anthony Cahill, consistent with him having discharged a firearm or coming into contact with one. On the soles of his black boots there were elongated grass marks, grey dust marks and white lime marks – the same as the material found at Smurfit's. The Walther PP automatic pistol recovered by the police had been recently fired.

On the soles of the boots there were fragments of glass, which had cut the upper leg portion of the boots. The glass was the same type as that found at the basement window of the flat in Raglan Road where they had tried to take cover. The motorbike had traces of dried blood. Fibres from Anthony's denims were found on the bike.

The evidence was enough to persuade the pair to plead guilty. In February 1979 Anthony and John Cahill were sentenced to ten years each for the Smurfit robbery. It would be Anthony's last conviction; he died of a drug overdose while in prison in the Curragh.

Quentin Flynn Robbery

29 JANUARY 1981: BY NOW MARTIN CAHILL WAS FREE AGAIN and determined not to let forensics gain any further ground on the activities of his criminal fraternity. He and Christy Dutton, a forty-four-year-old Ballyfermot criminal, walked into Quentin Flynn, a computer games business in an industrial estate in Clondalkin. Both were armed and masked. Dutton was wearing a three-piece suit, having just appeared in the District Court, where he was remanded on continuing bail on an assault charge. They pointed a gun at the secretary, Josephine Burke, who handed over more than £5,000. The pair made their getaway on a stolen black Kawasaki 750. Dutton was the pillion passenger.

Cahill had grown impatient waiting for Dutton to hop on the back and had revved the bike's engine so much that the exhaust pipe burned the shape of a cylinder groove into the soles and heels of Dutton's shoes, leaving a thick plastic skin on the exhaust pipe. As the pair neared home territory in Rathmines a routine garda patrol recognised the registration and began to follow them. After a high-speed chase the abandoned bike was found in Terenure. Shortly afterwards Cahill and Dutton were apprehended under the Offences Against the State Act. The two were held for forty-eight hours, by which time the money, which they had dumped in a ditch in Bushy Park, near the River Dodder, had been recovered.

On 31 January 1981 Martin Cahill and Christy Dutton were charged with armed robbery and the possession of firearms.

Among the items sent to me for analysis were Cahill's dark blue anorak with a multi-coloured stripe running down each sleeve, a wine-coloured cardigan with a blue diamond pattern on the front, a pair of his jeans, stained with mud in the front of the legs, a wine polo-neck sweater, a pair of brown shoes and socks and a black motorcycle helmet with a chin strap. From

Christy Dutton was taken a fawn-coloured suit, a leather belt, tie, shirt, socks, white vest, and a red, white and blue underpants; as well as his shoes, a black motorcycle helmet and a blue anorak with a broad green stripe down the sleeves. Both Cahill and Dutton had worn gloves. They had a *sliotar* (a hurling ball) in a pink cloth – a deadly weapon for breaking glass or cracking skulls.

When their belongings arrived I found that the heat damage on the shoes was consistent with the soles being in contact with the exhaust pipe of a motorcycle. The plastic on the exhaust pipe was the same type as that used in the sole of Dutton's shoes. There were flakes of reddish-brown paint on the shoes found in the ditch in Bushy Park. In all, I found fifty-eight pieces of evidence linking the pair to the stolen bike and to the site in Bushy Park where the money was recovered.

On 16 October 1981 Martin Cahill was returned for trial from the District Court to the Circuit Court. That night the office of the senior clerk, John Tidd, was broken into and Cahill's trial file was set on fire. The office was badly damaged. When that didn't succeed in stopping the trial and a new file was put in the Circuit Criminal Court, Cahill ordered his associates to set fire to the main Four Courts building. The fire caused extensive damage to the central chambers.

In November and December 1981 I had to go down to the partly gas-lit District Courthouse – the place where a suspect is first charged – on three different occasions to give my deposition in the ensuing case against Martin Cahill for the Quentin Flynn robbery. Cahill's legal team had already obtained a copy of my report when they applied for 'discovery', or access to all documents in the DPP's (Director of Public Prosecutions) case, as is normal. Nevertheless, I was called to the courtroom and put sitting in front of Cahill so that I could give my report verbally while the clerk transcribed what I was reading into longhand. Normally one would be called to give the deposition only once, but Cahill was deliberately frustrating due process by calling me to appear and then telling me I would not be required today. Three times I was summoned to court, only to be told that Mr Cahill would not be 'needing me' today. I was extremely frustrated that Cahill could abuse the system in this way and waste my time. The deposition I would give would not differ in any respect from the report already issued.

I was under no illusions but that Cahill was using this hold over me as a form of intimidation. But I began to worry that he might have some other sinister reason for making me appear in a certain place at a certain time. Had he planned to kill me there? As it turned out, I sensed his intention correctly; I just got the particulars of his plan wrong.

On the last such December afternoon, as I again went up the stairs leading to District Courts 14 and 15, expecting to read out my report, Cahill and Christy Dutton were coming down the courtroom steps. When they saw me, they burst out laughing. Apparently I was the most amusing thing they had ever seen. When I went up into the court I was told that Martin Cahill no longer required me. At the time I believed he was laughing at me because he had wasted my time again by lodging more legal applications to stall the taking of my deposition. I was wrong.

I was driving to work the following morning when an explosive device went off under my car. So, in fact what was amusing Cahill was that he believed this was the last time he would see me. He was laughing because he knew that I was about to lose my life and he would be responsible for taking it.

Detectives later informed me that on this first attempt, two English criminals planted the petrol bomb under my car at Cahill's behest and he oversaw the process. As it turned out, the device failed to explode properly and I managed to steer my car onto a grass verge on the left-hand side of the road near Newlands Cross. I had been moving at a very slow speed when the car sort of rose off the road. An amazing ball of flame lifted and almost supported it up. The flames came in through the dashboard and my car went out of control. I learned later that the type of device used had killed a number of people in Britain previously. I survived this attempt on my life, largely unhurt.

Although a wide variety of criminals were taking my findings personally, I knew Cahill was the one who had targeted me by planting the bomb in my car. That day on the steps of the District Court he had as good as let me know he was going to get me. And he had already established a pattern of wreaking retribution on anyone who tried to bring him to justice – the break-ins and fires in the courts were only a small proof of his vengeance.

And Cahill was determined to finish the job. On 6 January 1982, less than a month after his first attempt to kill me, he tried again.

7 January 1982, The Irish Times
IRA, INLA DENY ATTACK ON DONOVAN
Peter Murtagh, Security Correspondent

Criminal elements are suspected of having been behind the attempted assassination of the head of the Garda Siochána Forensic Science Laboratory, Dr James Donovan.

Spokesmen for the political wings of both the Provisional IRA and the INLA have denied that either organisation was involved.

Yesterday afternoon Dr Donovan underwent major surgery to his left leg but doctors at St James's Hospital in Dublin will not know for at least another 24 hours if his foot can be saved.

Dr Donovan's wife was with him before and after his operation.

Meanwhile gardaí investigating the assassination attempt began to sift through evidence which will shortly be used in the criminal trials in the hope of isolating someone who might have wanted Dr Donovan killed. A team of 40 detectives also carried out house-to-house checks of people in the Belgard Heights area of Tallaght where Dr Donovan lives.

Chief Superintendent John O'Driscoll, who is in charge of crime investigation in the

Dublin area, said last night that gardaí believe the bomb was attached to Dr Donovan's car early yesterday morning. However there is no indication yet as to who was responsible.

'We're keeping an open mind about it and checking a number of suspects,' he said.

In a statement the government promised that it would not shirk its responsibility to take any action that might be necessary to ensure the law was enforced. The attempt on Dr Donovan's life is the first incident in recent years in which someone has tried to murder a servant of the state other than a member of the Garda or Army and clearly the government views it very seriously.

'We will have to evaluate the seriousness of the incident, but that doesn't mean we will be any less determined,' the Minister for Justice, Mr Mitchell told The Irish Times last night. The attack was also condemned by the Fianna Fáil leader, Mr Haughey, who said the attack was reprehensible.

Dr Donovan will be incapacitated for several weeks and his absence is expected to severely disrupt the workings of the criminal courts, which begin hearing cases again next week after the Christmas recess. He was to have given evidence in them ...

A Government statement issued after the explosion said: 'Dr Donovan's work in the Forensic Science Laboratory has been of critical importance in the solution of a number of major crimes, including murder. There can be little doubt that today's outrage was connected with his work and the fear must be that it was a cold-blooded attempt to put an end to the effective functioning of the Forensic Science Laboratory in the solution of certain types of crimes and the apprehension of criminals.'

While I was lying in my hospital bed, evidence from the bombing started arriving into the Lab, piece by piece, and the reports passed on to me confirmed all of my suspicions. The bomb used on me was a crude homemade device, packed into a shaving foam container and strapped around the exhaust pipe of my car. It was designed to detonate when the heat in the tube was sufficiently high to cause the electric detonator to explode. In design it bore all the hallmarks of the car bombs being used in Northern Ireland, indicating the involvement of someone who was connected with the IRA or INLA (Irish National Liberation Army), but in the immediate aftermath both organisations denied any involvement. From their routine intelligence gathering, gardaí learned that Martin Cahill had a renegade INLA man plant the bomb. Cahill stood and kept watch – overseeing the process as he had done the first time.

THE DUEL RESUMES

First Meeting with Cahill after Assassination Attempt: The Quentin Flynn Trial

29 MAY 1984: I CAME FACE TO FACE WITH MARTIN CAHILL for the first time since the explosion, exactly two years and four months after the bomb destroyed my legs. It was for the resumed Quentin Flynn case trial and Cahill was pleading his innocence in the Clondalkin robbery. I was there to inform the jury of the evidence I had found linking him and his co-accused, Christy Dutton, to the scene. It included the grooves in the shoe soles made by the heat of the exhaust pipe on his motorbike, and the soil matches found in Bushy Park where the pair had stashed the loot during the getaway.

I have a tendency to dwell on things in advance and in my mind I had subconsciously built this day up. It had almost the same significance for me as if Cahill was finally standing trial for what he had done to me. The last time I had seen Cahill with Dutton, the pair were laughing hysterically at me on the steps of the courthouse and the next day the first device went off under my car. Now I felt it was my turn to be the one laughing – they thought they were never going to see me again, but I had survived.

Although detectives knew Cahill was behind the bombing and that he had also tinkered with the idea of abducting and shooting me, they discovered that he opted for the car bomb to feign an IRA attack because of the frequency with which they were being used in the North. But there was still not enough hard evidence to get him to court. The number of detectives assigned to my case immediately after the attack had now petered down to a handful, and out of the forty arrests made, nobody had been charged. When Martin Cahill was arrested in connection with the crime of blowing me up, he rubbed finger-print ink all over his face. I needed no further confirmation. In his own distorted way of looking at the world that was his lan-guage of confession.

I knew, as every crime investigator knows, that the longer time passed, the slimmer were my chances of ever getting justice. And Cahill was all the time growing shrewder. He was no longer taking part in armed robberies himself, but instead was overseeing them – planning them and supplying the weapons. Without trace evidence to link him to the scenes of the crime, proving his involvement beyond reasonable doubt was becoming next to impossible, especially given his reputation for silencing informers among the ranks of the underworld.

All these things were preying on my mind in the run-up to the trial. I was trying to apply a kind of scientific detachment in order to analyse what might happen in advance, so that I would at least be prepared. I knew that whenever Cahill found himself facing a brick wall he smashed it down. He had burned the District Court office. He tried to burn down the Four Courts. I felt it was reasonable to presume, therefore, that he might have another go at me.

Several times when I was recovering from the surgery on my legs after the explosion, ambulances and fire brigades and even a hearse would arrive at our door. I knew this was Martin Cahill's way of reminding me of the events of 6 January 1982. He was letting me know that what he had intended would come to pass. I believed he would strike again.

There is no dock in the Circuit Criminal Court and when I entered, Cahill was sitting on a bench with Dutton. Neither of them was handcuffed – one of the conveniences of being presumed innocent. I hobbled past them to get to the witness bench. There were just a few feet between us. I was aware that the gardaí in the court were moving protectively up behind me, and I knew then that my own fears about the direct physical threat weren't completely outlandish. My legs were still very painful; the original injuries had not yet healed but there was still a novelty factor, if you like, in that I still thought I would get better. If I had known then that twenty years later I would be in the same boat I honestly don't know if I could have entered that court.

Then a strange thing happened. Instead of being filled with fear, I was overwhelmed by some outside strength. The judge, Frank Martin, had been very solicitous of me, but it wasn't his kind words that buoyed me up. It was as if, when facing into the abyss and knowing all too well its horrors, I realised that no matter what else happened, nothing Cahill could do to me would touch my spirit.

My evidence lasted for two days, the trial itself only four. Everything I had learned about the body language of self-preservation – avoiding eye contact with the accused and so on – went out the window. I found myself wanting to look at Cahill so that he would be forced to look at me. But he resolutely refused to catch my eye. This was quite obvious to me, in the same way that someone whom you have caught staring suddenly looks actively away. He would look at the ground, or at the ceiling, but not at me. I don't know if that was a form of communication in itself but my impression grew, during the times I was addressing the judge or jury, that he was studying me then as my eyes were elsewhere. Yet each time I looked down at him, his face would jerk away. This made me more and more determined to force him to look me in the eye.

But if Martin Cahill could avoid being stared at, he had made sure the jury could not. In the courtroom he had placed a gang member for each juror, with instructions to stare and sneer at whichever one of the twelve jury members they had been assigned. It was pure, blatant intimidation and everyone in court could see it clearly. But even the prospect of influencing the verdict was too much of a gamble for Cahill who was unwilling to wait until it was delivered. Instead, he had the trial interrupted by gang members roaring from the balcony that he was only a murdering 'dirt bag drug dealer'. Judge Martin was wise to Cahill's attempt to collapse the trial and refused to abort. Instead he directed the jury to simply disregard what they had heard. It seemed that Cahill was on the verge of finally being thwarted and getting his come-uppance.

However, after the prosecution team had finished, counsel for Cahill and Dutton claimed that the State had not made the case that Josephine Burke, the Quentin Flynn company secretary, had been put in fear of her life during the robbery – a point of law on which the conviction for armed robbery hinged. Josephine Burke, when questioned on this point during the trial, had indicated that she was not in fear for her life during the incident. The trial fell apart. Cahill had once again slipped through the net. He gave gardaí the two fingers as he left court.

I was devastated, of course. I was thrown back in time to the day his brother Anthony had got away with John Copeland's murder, when the facts of guilt and innocence and all the work put in by so many to establish the difference seemed superfluous.

I suppose in my heart I knew that this was our last chance and it had passed. Cahill was like a particularly virulent strain of a virus that adapts and mutates to thwart the antibodies of its host so it cannot be extinguished. He had learned from the mistakes of a life in crime and he had changed his ways; he was educating himself and was no longer hands-on. Instead he was blooding new gang members on small-time gigs like petrol stations and shops in preparation for the larger hits like Russborough House and the O'Connor's jewellery warehouse heist. He had fashioned for himself the role of planner – deciding where to hit – and fixer: the one who got the maps, provided the initial start-up capital, and solved problems thrown up in the course of executing his plot. This made him every bit as culpable as the gang members who carried it out, but harder to catch. It also made him more dangerous, because when he wasn't unknowingly leaving behind forensic evidence invisible to the naked eye, he was unstoppable.

Everybody in the courtroom on 29 May had, in their own way, recognised his dominance – whether it was the gardaí forming a human shield around me, or the judge recognising his attempts to collapse the trial. And, of course, Cahill did dominate; he ran rings around procedure.

Yet, all the while, he was portrayed and perceived in the public arena as a sort of buffoon or clown. That really stung me. I always felt that by not taking him seriously, people weren't taking me seriously either. If, after all, the public believed him harmless, how could they then believe him capable of harming me? To make sense of this, I likened the public desire to reduce the seriousness of who and what he was to what was going on in Northern Ireland. So many people were saying, Yes, I don't agree with violence, but ... The 'yes but-ers' were effectively condoning what was going on because they had given themselves an opt-out clause. In the absence of any moral leadership to show the 'yes but-ers' up for what they were, what they have been and what they always would be, people kept dying, thus perpetuating the violence. Similarly, in my own situation, Martin Cahill was being tolerated because 'yes' he was a gangster 'but' he was a real Dub as well. It does, in the end, come down to what the people want. You can see the true extent of people power when mobilised in the aftermath of the Veronica Guerin murder. Then the public had no reservations about the character of the people responsible for killing her. The ironic thing is that when compared to Cahill, this gang was small-time. But after the murder of the investigative journalist in 1996, it became clear that the law was inadequate and the public made it morally incumbent on politicians to effect change. Hence the legislation setting up the Criminal Assets Bureau and the Witness Protection Scheme.

But this is a media age. The media has the power to make 'The General', Martin Cahill, likeable and other criminals not. In so doing it influences the agenda in every government department. Evil men are continually made less threatening in the mind of the public by being given cartoon nicknames: The Coach, The Monk, The Psycho, The Viper, The Zombie, The Boxer, The Banker, The Colonel, The Builder, Mr Big, Fatso, The Penguin, The Tosser, etc. Cahill was depicted as a great laugh because he liked to show off his Mickey Mouse boxer shorts, and that made him somehow tolerable.

After Cahill got off on the Quentin Flynn charges, there were so many other things vying for my attention that my concentration was elsewhere. It was an age that saw the proliferation of heroin and other drugs on to the market and drug-related cases were placing an incredible strain on the Lab's resources. Apart from Cahill's crew, the country did not have established criminal gang networks in place, and so families like the Dunnes were literally filling the vacuum. Cahill got his early tuition in their stomping ground.

The Murder of Martin Cahill

THURSDAY, 18 AUGUST 1994: I WAS IN THE LAB WHEN Garda Inspector Gerry O'Carroll rang with the news that Martin Cahill was dead. He told me that five minutes earlier Martin Cahill had been shot and killed. My reaction was one of huge relief. Apart from the havoc he had already wreaked in my life, there had been recent indications that he might be preparing to strike again. Just two months before he died, he was regularly loitering outside my home. I would arrive home from work and neighbours would say, 'We don't want to worry you but that man in the anorak was here again.' My wife became afraid to open the front door. Now he was dead and that particular threat was removed.

Cahill's end came because he thought he was invincible. I think it fair to presume he must also have been losing his grip on reality. Everyone who lived in Ireland through the 1970s and 1980s knew what the IRA were capable of, yet he thought he could taunt them as he had the State. He refused to play their game and developed contacts among Loyalist paramilitaries, to whom he sold several paintings stolen from the Beit collection. He was on safer grounds defying the State – justice has rules but terrorism has none.

CHAPTER 2:
AN ORDINARY DECENT CRIMINAL
Debunking the Myth

OCCASIONALLY PEOPLE HAVE TRIED TO COMFORT ME by suggesting that what happened to me has made me privy to the darker side of human nature, and therefore makes me better at what I do. I don't understand this rationale. The real puzzle of suffering is of course its arbitrariness: why do the innocent suffer, and not the guilty? Why do men of utterly evil intent, like Martin Cahill, escape the suffering that is meted out to their victims? Cahill had a healthy life, barring his bad diet, which he could have changed. He amassed a fortune in stolen goods: artworks from the Beit collection, which he was singularly incapable of appreciating, and a treasure trove of jewellery courtesy of O'Connor's warehouse. He had several houses, enjoyed the love of several women, and had hoards of cash buried all over the place. And in the end, Cahill's death was swift and clean. What more can any man ask for?

I know I have no right to expect justice from the street when the courts never convicted anyone for what happened to me.

Despite all the forensic evidence I have gathered in my time, in my own case there was not enough evidence to convict Cahill and, in garda terms, it remains an unsolved crime. But right until his end, nothing could stop this man from imposing himself in the most menacing fashion imaginable into my life.

You will understand why then, at the very least, Cahill's death came as a great relief. However, the glorification of his life, posthumously, was a totally unexpected phenomenon. Three films have been made about his 'accomplishments' – *The General, Ordinary Decent Criminal* and *Vicious Circle.* To add insult to injury, in March 2001 RTÉ screened all three as part of an 'Ireland on Screen' season, raising Cahill to new representative heights.

I speak only for myself when I say that the reincarnation of Cahill as a 'crook with a heart of gold' has been even more hurtful than his original crime. But I am by no means the only casualty: Brian Purcell, the social welfare official brave enough to sign Cahill off the dole, was knee-capped for doing his job. Two people who happened to live above a fast-food restaurant at 24 Leeson Street barely escaped with their lives after Cahill set fire to the building in the early hours of the morning because it was 'taking' business from his own hot-dog stall. And a German fast food entrepreneur, Wolfgang Eullitz, who ran *The Hungry Wolf* restaurant in the basement of 74 Leeson Street, was shot in the leg for refusing to give in to his demand for protection money. Detective Superintendent Ned Ryan lived under the shadow of death after Cahill put a contract on his life. Cahill's elderly neighbours in Cowper Downs were intimidated on a daily basis but stood up to him in their own silent but stoic way – albeit in utter terror – by refusing to move house. In return, he dumped his household rubbish into their garden on a daily basis, slashed the neighbourhood's tyres indiscriminately, sat on garden walls peering into their home for hours on end and shone torches into their windows in the middle of the night.

Even among his own cronies there were victims – one of his gang was nailed to a wooden floor when suspected of 'diverting' gold that was being transported to a fence in England. Another, David Lynch, a heroin addict, was dumped by Cahill out of the getaway car when returning from the robbery of a doctor's surgery in Carlow, because he had overdosed. Cahill made sure to remove the man's shoes so he could not be forensically linked to the scene. He left the twenty-six-year-old to die alone in a windswept car park at the top of Mount Leinster near the RTÉ transmitter. Even Cahill's dog was kept permanently tied up and was a pathetic sight that anybody with any strain of mercy would have treated more humanely.

Yet all three of the films portrayed him as an amusing kind of character, a real Dub, and a sort of latter-day 'Robin Hood'– ignoring the reality of his life and crimes. Take, for instance, the twelve-year-old girl who was raped and buggered by her father, one of Cahill's gang members, in 1992. The child's mother was dead and she was sleeping with an older sister because she was living in fear of her father. But that didn't stop him. After her ordeal the girl told her grandmother everything. She brought the child to hospital and informed the father that his daughter had given a statement to the gardaí. He was arrested and charged on five counts of incest. Martin Cahill was furious; he and the gang member had been planning the kidnapping of National Irish Bank's Jim Lacey and the last thing they needed was to be the focus of garda attention. Cahill followed the girl as she walked from her grandmother's house to the shops. He offered her £20,000 and a new life in England if she withdrew the charges. When she refused, he had 'tout' daubed on her grandmother's house and shone torches in the windows at night. He also threatened to kill the girl's uncle. In a final bid to stop the trial, Cahill shot his accused friend in the leg. The trial was postponed but when it went ahead, the criminal was found guilty and sentenced to ten years. In the film, *The General*, the girl is played by a much older, fully-developed female actress , adding years to her true age in the minds of the viewers. This plays down the nastiness of Cahill's involvement and is grossly unfair to a pre-pubescent child who either out of strength or naivety stood up to Cahill's attempts to intimidate her and bribe her out of giving evidence.

Cahill also supplied John Gilligan – the man found not guilty by the Special Criminal Court of organising the murder of Veronica Guerin – with half a million pounds to 'break-into' the lucrative heroin market in the early 1990s. Gilligan is now serving twenty-eight years, the longest ever prison sentence handed out by the Irish courts for drug dealing. Yet the films maintain that Cahill had nothing to do with drugs, although gardaí suspect that he himself supplied his own brother Anthony with his last fatal fix while visiting him in the Curragh prison. Also he had robbed phenobarbitone, mogadon, philorphin and cyclimorph, all in injection form, from the surgery in Carlow – hardly for his own use.

The effect of this so-called artistic licence is to hammer into history the idea that Cahill was a 'victim of society', provoked into violence and forced to engage in a battle of wits with detectives. By transforming him from a vengeful and self-absorbed criminal, who maimed and killed people, into a diabolically clever Super Hero, gifted in armed and unarmed combat, who only 'hurt' those who deserved it, his image is ripe for imitation.

Perhaps you will understand a little better now why I cannot consider Cahill's litany of butchery as the work of some great military commander who has earned the rank and title of 'General'. What I still fail to grasp is why a society would deliberately glorify a man who despised it.

I cannot bring myself round to calling Cahill 'The General', as the media would have liked. It implies a level of social responsibility which he lacked completely. But I never underestimated him. On the contrary, as an adversary he was a very able man. He was reared in Dublin tenements by a mother who was pregnant eighteen times, but he refused to let his start in life consign him to the poverty trap and ended up presiding over a crime empire with a turnover of £20 million. The point is that he and I were diametrically opposed. Where I devoted my life to maintaining the State, he was committed to its demolition. The State had used its strongest tools upon him – the church, reform school, prison, and the new tool at its disposal – forensic science – and he was bent on getting even.

He robbed the office of the DPP of Books of Evidence on which pending trials depended and files containing the names of garda informants. He took the files on the death of Fr Niall Molloy and on the notorious Malcolm McArthur for his own personal reading material.

He set the Four Courts and the Chief State Solicitor's office on fire and plundered the invaluable Beit art collection from the nation's heritage.

And all the while, on his nocturnal prowls, he was creating his own sub-State, an underworld equipped with his own private army. He managed to unify Dublin's most notorious criminals into the most dangerous gang the country has ever known.

CHAPTER 3:
THE CAHILL LEGACY
Life Since the Explosion

AFTER THE FIREMEN CUT ME FROM THE BODYWORK of my bombed car I was rushed to St James's Hospital where surgeons immediately began to repair the extensive damage to my lower legs, reassembling the lower halves, and replanting my severed left foot. There was also uncertainty as to whether my eyesight would return. An x-ray of the right eye found my cornea had been extensively scarred by shrapnel particles. Thankfully, none had passed through the eye and into the brain.

Over the next eighteen months I required ten operations on my foot alone. It was not an easy procedure. The bones had to be reduced and fixed in position. Since there are 103 bones in a foot, each of which moves with every step, all the internal structures needed tending to and a foot-like object – partly my own foot reconstructed, partly prosthetic – was fashioned in its place. I also required skin grafts, which created new injuries and pain in other areas, something I was quite unprepared for. However, the leg was saved.

I spent about seven weeks in hospital following the explosion during which time I was in surgery almost every second day. On the days I went to theatre it was not possible to eat anything, and on the alternate days the combination of pain, drugs and the unreal atmosphere meant I could not eat either. My weight plummeted to under seven stone. The nurses started feeding me from the doctor's canteen because there is more protein in the medics' diet. But I don't believe it was the lack of food that was causing the wasting.

My room was exceptionally stark, the only window situated just under the ceiling. I seldom glimpsed my legs but when I did my vision was totally absorbed by the huge metal contraption on my bed. Metal hoops encirled my limbs; from each leg three long needle spokes protruded and connected to the hoops. Roughly packed around this contraption were the devastated remains of my bone and tissue, pressed back together by net and gauze. The spokes were corked at the top, to stop the sheets catching, and the mere sight of such a basic little anti-friction invention was enough to make me minimise movement. This in turn caused me to develop pressure (bed) sores.

I was growing more and more depressed at my situation. They were amputating more and more pieces from the ends of my legs. The outside of what remained of my left foot had been entirely replaced by a skin graft, but without any tissue to provided padding for my weight, it became very tender and regularly broke down. My foot was unsightly and constantly infected. I was tired of the whole process and of the hospital environment. What I really wanted was to go home with my wife who was at my bedside from the very first moment the news was broken to her, even while residents closest to the scene of the explosion were still putting the sound of the bomb down to blasting in the nearby Roadstone factory. She has stood by me through everything – even when it meant her own life came under threat. The bomb changed the entire course of her life as well as mine. We did not have a family when it detonated. Looking back it was probably just as well. My wife has never once asked me to give up my job and for that I am profoundly grateful. If she had asked, what choice would I have had?

I was out of work for four months during which time I could think of nothing but that I would one day have to return. It worried me that as a disabled man I might not be able to do so and sickened me that Martin Cahill had taken away even my right to choose my future. But I knew that I could not let him win and leave the Forensic Laboratory, which was still in its infancy. If I went, how could I expect the rest of the staff to stay on – like sitting ducks? That was something which for a long time I was unable or unwilling to face. It was hard enough to come to terms with what had happened.

After four months I received a 'gentle reminder' from the Department: that a civil servant who takes sick leave for more than six months goes on half pay and their job cannot be guaranteed. Everything is black and white in the Civil Service.

So I returned to work. As it happened, the caseload in the Forensic Lab was now at such a level that it needed a full-time administrator to manage the work. But for the explosion and my injuries, I might have hung on a bit longer on active casework, but as it was I went into full-time administration.

To equip my mind with a way to manage the physical pain caused by my injuries, I have tried a myriad of treatments. I have taken courses in esoteric philosophy, which taught me to live in the moment and not to resist suffering by dwelling on what happened in the past or what might be waiting in the future. To do so ruins the present. Nor can you retreat from pain or resist it when it comes. That causes the whole body to contract, which accentuates the discomfort. Esoteric philosophy says that if you allow your whole body to accept that you are one with pain, the life force within you will stimulate healing and regeneration. I have to say this way of thinking did help to ease the pain somewhat.

But all treatments need you to believe in them, because faith brings hope. I went to faith healers because I believed that the compassion of one human being could bridge the remove at which I found myself after another human being had set out to destroy me. The theory behind the laying-on of hands is that another person's energy can clear the blockages in a victim's energy. Acupuncture acts in the same way and I tried it too.

In 1993 I attempted electro-magnetism therapy at a pain clinic in Ballsbridge. A battery was attached to both sides of the knees and an electric current passed by electrode to scramble the pain signals coming up the legs. The idea is to use electricity to stimulate blood flow, using a 'TENS' (transcutaneous electrical nerve stimulation) machine. Magnets attempt to stimulate the nerves under the skin to bring blood to the vital area.

In March 1996 I began another 'alternative' pain therapy: having a 'sympathetic block' injected in my spine while under general anaesthetic. I had injections in June, August and September of 1996; in May and September of 1997 and five between March and September of 1998. The process had to be stopped because I started experiencing severe weakness in the legs and a major drop in blood pressure on awakening.

From July 1997 to April 1998 I attended an endorphin clinic in Dublin every fortnight. Endorphins are pain-reducing hormones released by the brain which were stimulated by applying pressure to the damaged areas. It helped but I found it too uncomfortable to continue.

I had boots specially made by two different clinics to rectify balance, and prosthetic insoles inserted to cradle the rigid contours at the end of the legs, but they press and pinch the flesh and cause abscesses. All of this made me seriously contemplate amputation. In 1998 surgeons suggested I attend an orthopaedic hospital to see the conditions of amputees because they felt I was placing too much emphasis on amputation to remove pain. They wanted me to know precisely the problems that can arise after removal of the legs.

But the thing which I continue to find most distressing about my injuries is the constant breakdown of tissue under the legs, causing considerable oozing of matter and blood. When this happens, the legs have to be dressed daily. I wear two pairs of socks and each night check the inner pair for signs of blood. Sometimes the wounds develop enormous calluses and a few times a week have to be soaked and rasped off. This does not stop the infections growing and bleeding into the calluses, which causes hideous black areas.

I know that some of these details may be disturbing to readers but I think it is important to know exactly what happens when one human being tries to eliminate another; important not just for myself but for all victims of violence. So often we see victims of terrible acts of inhumanity as a one-day feature in a newspaper. Then they are forgotten by all but their family and carers, even though they may have to endure a life sentence of suffering. For a criminal, a life sentence usually means ten years at the most.

During 1998, besides the normal breakdowns, a large erosion started under the left leg and developed into an open wound with that distinctive odour of decaying tissue I had long ago associated with my father's ulcers. It was possible to see deep within the wound, which was very disturbing – like peering into one's own mortality. While a number of consultants were sceptical about the wound ever healing, the plastic surgeon who reassembled my foot after the explosion was successful in treating this new injury. But he warned me that I could never again afford to allow a wound to fester or the result would be catastrophic.

To make matters worse, just as I had got over this set-back, a flange of new bone started growing along the outside of my newly-formed left heel. I was due to have it surgically removed because it was upsetting my balance and distressing to look at, but I accidentally slipped on the stairs at home and fractured my leg. I was rushed by ambulance to a local hospital, where I was diagnosed as having a 'congenital deformity' of the lower legs! The fracture was not diagnosed until several days later by a surgeon in another hospital; the delay severely exacerbated the break. Apart from the mental trauma of knowing I was in severe pain and being told nothing was wrong, there was the added physical problem of the swelling pulling apart the wounds I had sustained in the explosion nineteen years earlier. The result was extreme blistering, which developed into enormous bags of infected water that hung from the heel, which kept bursting and filling again. I was in agony. At my wits end, from January 2000, I had fifteen sessions of Reiki treatment, the only pain therapy I had tried which does not require you to believe in it. Reiki is an ancient Japanese therapy that invites the life force of the universe to engulf the mind, body and spirit. But again under instruction to lie still, I had to accept I could not master pain, I was its slave.

In January 1999 I chose the most dramatic of all the treatments and had a spinal cord stimulator inserted in my back that required two separate operations and the signing of a disclaimer should I be paralysed during the procedure, which has happened on occasion. The night before the operation, the woman lying in the room next to me started to scream endlessly because she had changed her mind. I knew how she felt and was seriously considering doing the same. The only thing that held me back was that in my case all other options had been exhausted. And the risk proved worth it. The procedure was extremely delicate, requiring that I be kept awake and fully conscious to verify that the spine was not being damaged. In the first operation, five electrodes were hammered into my spine and a lead taken from them and brought through my body where it was connected to a battery. Some days later I had a second operation to connect the lead to a receiver and battery which sits inside my waist on my left side. I control the pain by adjusting the pulses of electricity through the spine. I must admit I have noticed a real difference. The increased blood to my legs has improved the quality of tissue considerably and it is no longer rotting the way it used to. It's as if, finally, the blood vessels have been fooled into opening up again.

For the first time in twenty years I am beginning to feel a little better. I have had other, unrelated illnesses like anyone else: irritable bowel syndrome, asthma, arthritis, and the most recent being skin cancer, diagnosed in December 1998. When I had spent so many years trying to preserve flesh it was ironic that for the cancer treatment I had to have pieces of skin burned off. But I can accept disease as part of life, and God's will is a lot easier to cope with than a criminal's.

My injuries have had a domino effect on the rest of my health. The side effects of taking painkillers have included the erosion of my oesophagus, which causes a permanent burning sensation in my throat, and the ulceration of the upper stomach, which has meant restrictions on my diet. To combat these side-effects, I was prescribed 40mg of the drug Losec in 1992. The maximum prescription period recommended by the manufacturers is eight weeks, but eight years later I am still on this drug, which inhibits the generation of acid, needed for the uptake of nutrients, especially Vitamin C, from the diet.

It is in the little things that I learn how much more the able-bodied man's life is worth. When I take a flight, I am moved from whichever seat I may have been first allocated to a window seat – always the one furthest from the emergency exit – presumably so that an able-bodied passenger, even supposing they were a criminal, or drunk, can escape unimpeded. Why? Should a plane plunge from the sky and its huge hulk of metal swirl under the surface of the ocean, the disabled will have as much chance as the able-bodied. Water does not discriminate.

In June 1994 my wife and I went to Lisbon on holidays. Our first morning away was memorable, not just because of the city's incredible beauty, but also because my wife and I were mugged in the underground. I fell down in the mêlée and was trying to drag myself back up when I glimpsed my wife caught between the two muggers and fighting vigorously with a third who was trying to rip her bag from her shoulder. The incident ended without serious injury but twice more on that holiday we were singled out for attack, once as we approached a cathedral to visit some saint's body and again on the underground. I learned later that drugtaking had become a massive problem in Lisbon, and that addicts desperate for their next fix had turned to bag-snatching as a ready source of funds. However, at the time I remember thinking that, but for Martin Cahill, I would be able-bodied and not considered such an obvious soft target.

Even now, every day I am reminded of what has been done to me. Each morning as I get up I must remember to get out of bed at the right angle so as not to overbalance and fall down; before I return to bed I must peel off blood-soaked socks and inspect new festering ulcers. Should I stay in bed, my circulation hits a virtual standstill and stalls any prospect of healing. And when I sit in a wheelchair, the world is a foreign place. People do not look me in the eye. It is as though as a disabled man I have become a harbinger of ill fate, as if, somewhere deep down, people believe contact with the afflicted is somehow contagious.

I have not been equipped with any platform to easily forgive the man who did this to me. From a conservative Roman Catholic background like mine, suffering is God's will. But I draw no comfort from the fact that I am supposed to be in purgatory on earth – doing time, so to speak. I have seen what men who do real time are capable of doing to each other, but what crime did I commit befitting such punishment? I was simply doing my job.

Before this happened I had a strong faith. I have a degree in theology. But after the assassination bid, the bible offered me no answers, only platitudes. To tell me I will be rewarded in the next life is to insult the value of my present life which every day is eroded further.

Nearly twenty years on, you might say that I am beached on the shores of life. That is what living with constant physical pain means. Fear is the only thing more powerful – the thought that the pain will not end, that relief will never come. The need to construct a timeframe is all-consuming. I know when the pain began but not that it will end.

People say I should try to forget, to put what happened behind me, to move on. But everything about my waking existence today revolves around that moment in time, that day in 1982 when Martin Cahill set out to deliberately rip me apart. If I am bitter about him, and I am, perhaps it is understandable, given the legacy he has left me.

CHAPTER 4:
THE FATES OF THE JIM DONOVANS

I WAS NAMED AFTER MY UNCLE AND GRANDFATHER, both Jim Donovan, and in hindsight their unfortunate demises seemed to ominously foreshadow my own destiny. I had plenty of time for reflection of this sort during my hospitalisation and recovery after the bombing.

At thirty-six years of age and facing the prospect of life without a leg, I began to see patterns in my childhood in Cork City that brought me full circle to this point in time. It seemed to me that violence had run like an invisible artery throughout the entire course of my life. However, I fully accept that this may have been the effects of the morphine!

No two cities are exactly the same. From overhead, each lattice of streets is as specific as a fingerprint. Among the whorls of terraces that coil around Cork City is Cattle Market Street, where I was born on 16 July 1944. My homeplace was very close to the North Cathedral and Shandon, where Jack Lynch was from. People were very proud of him and my uncles boasted that they had played hurling within him in school.

Cork's tradition of service in the British army and navy

endured in the aftermath of the First World War even as republican fundamentalism soared to fever pitch, and this set it apart
from its neighbouring counties. Perhaps this is the reason why,
in the course of my career, I have never believed that a sectarian
cause ever outweighs the human cost of an atrocity.

My parents married late in life, having worked in England
during the Second World War. I remember as a child walking
with my father, Michael, through Grand Parade and him stopping at the cenotaph to point out the names of two of the war
dead on the list, both named Watson. He announced with pride
that the men were his uncles and my great-uncles. So, although
the main function of schooling at that time was to make us all
confirmed republicans, perpetually lamenting the loss of 'the
fourth green field', I did not think of England as the enemy at
all.

Cattle Market Street led up to Blarney Street, which prided
itself on being the longest street in Europe at the time. But when
I was small I could no more calculate its length than that of a pig
intestine before it was uncoiled in my grandfather's butcher
shop – Long's Butchers – on Douglas Street.

Even as a child, the stench of death clung to everything. It
had a day: Wednesday, when my uncle Gus would slaughter
and skin the animals in the abattoir attached to my grandfather's shop. This was the only time Gus would sing – on
Wednesdays when he was slaughtering and skinning and
taking intestines out. Somehow, to me as a child, music lessened the barbarism of the act. I remember that he had a perfectly pitched tenor's voice, which I presume he modelled on
the Italian opera companies visiting Cork in the 1920s and
1930s. Dublin did not have an Opera House, so Cork rejoiced in

having the upper hand.

But the sound of death could not be drowned out. The squeal of pigs would follow me through a lane off Gerald Griffin Street and seep into my ears in the classroom of the North Presentation school. As a youngster, death was not alien or foreign (although I have to admit I have never since been partial to pork). It provided labour in Dillon's Gut Factory. Nobody complained about the summertime stench of innards from this factory, situated exactly opposite my home. People were so glad of the work, even when it involved collecting the slops – bellies that had gone green – on a donkey and cart. Later, as an adult studying toxicology, those smells came back to me when dealing with cadavers.

Across the road from my infant school in Blackpool was a factory belonging to Denny's, the sausage manufacturers, that also gave the area a very distinctive smell. In the morning break, I remember Sister Eucharia giving me milk and bread and jam, something provided only for children who were poor, or, as in my case, sickly. My mother had her own notion of what was good for me, and during lunchbreak when I was in primary school she would give me a 'ponney' (enamel cup) containing a mix of half milk and half Murphy's stout, bought by the jug from the pub across the road. This 'tonic' may have been doing me good, but I'm afraid I didn't appreciate it!

Back then death was utterly intrinsic to everyday life, a reason to plant tansy flowers to mix into the bullocks' blood and improve the taste of that famous Cork delicacy, drisheen. I recall my grandfather dying, how as he lingered on the entire household was absorbed. Even then I understood that the tableau effect created by his prostrate body lying on white sheets –

like a slab in a morgue – surrounded by my mother and aunts, was somehow filled with ceremony.

Death was not selective; it struck at random all around us. One of my classmates died from rickets and several from bronchial related illnesses: pneumonia, tuberculosis (TB), asthma. I have no recollection of anyone reacting with outrage to these young deaths, being scandalised or ever sensing that it could or should have been in any way prevented. It would have been like trying to force back the tide. I do remember the sense of shame exuded by the families of those who had died young of TB. I suppose this was because it was known that the bacterium could be carried on the breath. The families were fearful that they would be treated like lepers and considered contagious. You have to remember that in those days people relied for their survival on being part of the community. Ostracisation carried its own death sentence. I have deliberately never read Frank McCourt's Pulitzer Prize-winning book, *Angela's Ashes*, because it sounded too painfully comparable to the conditions of my own childhood. Decay was within and without: inside the body and outside in the crumbling tenements. I remember families being taken over by a new head of the household after fathers died or simply walked away, unable to cope with the huge demands placed upon them. What I have heard about McCourt's black humour on death and disease would also ring a bell. I remember clearly that there was a widespread fascination with constipation, as if that subject had immense relevance. There was a whole host of remedies for it, almost as many as there were for baldness!

There were other links that brought me from my stay in St James's Hospital back to boyhood. As I grappled with the news that I would never walk properly again, let alone run, I was returned to my childhood, when running was forbidden because I had chronic asthma. A child who cannot run is like a fish on the shore. I longed to explore the clustered maze that was Cork City. But in the radiating furls of the city's lanes and alleys, the rattle of my lungs was amplified by the heave of altitude. The sound of my breath bouncing off the dank, sodden, consumptive stairwell walls was like a warning bell to my mother, who confined me to the great indoors.

I remember the surprise of seeing her weeping after the doctor diagnosed my condition. My mother, Eileen Long, was a massive woman, over six feet tall and she must have weighed around eighteen stone. She was one of a family of ten children, and not easily shaken. She was the head of our household.

My mother's ailment was high blood pressure, which induced a swelling of the ankles. Each morning she would delight in displaying her trim new fetlocks. Each night they would have returned to their distended state. Although she was always on a diet, it was never a diet in the strict sense of the word. Warnings about the dangers of having more children were ignored with the same abandon, because of a greater duty to God. In 1949 she gave birth to identical twin girls, my little sisters – Helen and Carmel.

Of all the conditions and complaints that could be acquired in the 1940s, Cork was no place for wheezes and coughs. My father's only sister had died at the age of twelve from TB. And so when, at the age of five, my piano-accordion chest, which could whistle and play quite independent of the air pumped through it, was diagnosed as double pneumonia, I was brought to the sanatorium in the Bon Secours Hospital, effectively to die. That first experience with a hospital room was not at all pleasant. Back then I was also confined to the bed, and this was another reason why I so resented my second enforced stay. I began to believe that I was, as the family prophesied very early on, cursed by the legacy of my name.

My grandfather, Jim Donovan Snr, was crushed to death against the side of an ocean liner at the age of seventy. Like most men born in Cobh in the early nineteenth century, he had joined the British navy. Towards his latter years he had become a pilot for the White Star shipping line. His job was to board off-shore liners and steer the vessels into port for the transatlantic captain unfamiliar with the navigation of the harbour. In 1912 my grandfather piloted the *Titanic* and in 1915 the *Lusitania*. When the *Lusitania* was torpedoed by a German U-boat on 7 May 1915, killing 1,198 passengers and crew, he was also involved in bringing back the bodies. On the day of his death, my grandfather was climbing a rope ladder up the hull of a liner when a great wave lashed the boat from which had just disembarked and he was crushed between the two vessels.

My uncle, another Jim Donovan, also met an untimely end. On emigrating to the United States in 1927, he became a police-man in Boston. With only one month to go before he was due to retire from the force, he was stabbed to death after surprising two white youths who were breaking into a car.

Despite these dire portents, I did not die as my name bequeathed. But I endured terrible loneliness and a sense of abandonment. Although double pneumonia is not contagious, I was in a sanatorium and therefore in quarantine. I was allowed no visitors and had no form of entertainment; the nurses were afraid they would be unable to settle me if I played with toys. I would have given anything for a book and perhaps that is why I became such an avid reader when I was eventually released.

In my work I often come across cases where an impoverished childhood or deprivation is used as an argument for a criminal's actions. But I, and many other law-abiding people, knew poverty every bit as well as many of those criminals. I was brought up at a time when people lived in extremely cramped tenement conditions. The huge public estates of McSwiney's Villas were beginning to spring up near where I lived; green fields were being transformed into massive council housing estates like Gurranabraher and Farranree, with all the social problems associated with high percentages of unemployment. But we still had a strong sense of community, not an abhorrence of it. People cared about each other.

There was also an emphasis on self-betterment. Parents wanted your life to be better than theirs had been. I was raised to believe that I had as much right to take my place under the sun as any man, be he rich or titled or immensely talented. My mother instilled this into me, I presume because it had been denied to her. In her youth she had wanted to be a nurse, but a sister who had gone before her to London for training had eloped instead, and her father was not willing to squander his money a second time. So my mother, lamenting the fact that the size of her shoulders was directly proportionate to the size of her cross, projected her aspirations on me and offered up her lost education for her sins. Instead, she launched herself into the Roman Catholic faith with great fervour and consistency and accepted that she would have to make do with her lot.

I mention such things because all these influences weighed

heavily on what I would become in later life. I applied for and went to University College Cork in 1962, although I know at the time people wondered why, since there was no family tradition of third-level education and we were not wealthy. My first choice would have been medicine but that subject was very much on a pedestal and, since I was not a doctor's son, the sense that I would have been reaching too high above my station was too strong to overcome. There was also the worry of funding seven years in college, although, as it turned out, I ended up acquiring a PhD that took longer and was as expensive. In any event, I decided to read chemistry and physics for the simple reason that the subjects fascinated me; they explained things. Why was light white? How could it split into colours? How did one measure the speed at which it was travelling?

It was in college that I met my future wife. She was also from Cork, but from a farming background, and our lives took remarkably similar paths. We both did the same degree in Chemistry and qualified in 1966; both went on to do a PhD in much the same area of organic chemistry – the study of how things are made synthetically, such as drugs from plants. We both got jobs together in the State Laboratory in 1971. But that same year when we decided to marry, the marriage bar meant that she had to give up her career in the Civil Service and find a new job. It seems hard to believe now, but in those days married women (unless they were widows) were not allowed to work in the Civil Service. They were different times.

By night, I studied theology, I suppose in order to process the new wave of ideas that I was being exposed to while in University and to understand why my mother's faith was also my own, since Roman Catholicism often infuriated me. My first summer job as a teenager had been in a library where pages of books containing bad language would be ripped out by readers, something which I considered a disgrace. Even worse, if the words 'Christ' or 'Jesus' or 'sex' occurred, the books were simply removed from the shelves. It seemed an extremely greedy way of acting, to deprive somebody else of the right to make up their own mind. But the concept of freedom of expression didn't exist then and sex was never a topic of conversation, although my mother had a saying that she uttered many, many times, that: 'A man has to be dead at least three days before a woman is safe from him!' On Sunday nights, when RTÉ used to broadcast a play, she wouldn't let me listen because it was too crude or vulgar so instead I became quite a fan of Max Jaffa conducting the Palm Court Orchestra in the Grand Hotel on BBC Light!

*   *   *

So, although in many ways my childhood and the inherited ill-luck of my given name seemed to predestine me for an early grave, I escaped that fate – just about.

PART TWO
WITNESS PROTECTION AND THE JUSTICE SYSTEM

WITNESSES ARE VITAL for the operation of the judicial system. Crime is not going to go away but witnesses certainly have every reason to do so under the present system, and my belief is that unless something is done about protecting them, they will simply refuse to cooperate. I feel very strongly about this, having seen all too often in the courts how witnesses can be put in fear of their lives.

I recall one case involving a robbery in Annagry, County Donegal, in which the accused men were convicted on the basis of the evidence of one Patrick Gallagher, a very small, thin, frail-looking man with the heart of a lion. He was a very good witness in that his evidence was crisp and clear and without embroidery, and it secured both a prosecution and his fate. When Gallagher returned home after the trial, he was knee-capped on the side of the road. The bullets totally shattered his knees, making it impossible for him to walk. He tried to drag himself along the road to get help but he was bleeding profusely. On 1 June 1980 he died from his injuries. The message was unambiguous and intended to resonate amongst the community: evidence against certain groups would exact the full wrath of their revenge.

Secrecy and anonymity are very useful in the protection of witnesses. That secrecy exists nowadays in absolute form in the Family Law Courts and in Tribunals of Inquiry and Coroners' Courts, where evidence can be taken in secret. Witnesses in criminal cases deserve the same protection or they will simply not make themselves available to the courts for much longer.

There is a perception that the tradition of law in Ireland is somehow immutable; that things have always been done in the same way, and that to extend secrecy and anonymity to criminal cases does not fit into the scheme of things. But major changes have already been made. During the Second World War, Eamon de Valera set up military courts in Portlaoise to try subversives; in 1972 Jack Lynch created the Special Criminal Court after the murder of Garda Fallon, when it was obvious that convictions in terrorist cases had become impossible because of intimidation of juries. And then there are the dramatic changes in procedures relating to the hearing of family law cases.

The tribunals are another case in point. The Tribunals Act has effectively given tribunals the power to oblige a witness to answer questions to the satisfaction of the judges. If the answers are unsatisfactory and the witness is deemed not to be cooperating, then a term in prison may be imposed. Yet, in a criminal case, a defendant may be suspected of rape or murder and can still refuse to answer garda questions or to give a cheek swab for DNA analysis.

Eventually the Criminal Courts will also have to move with the times and allow some work to be done behind the scenes. Why should witnesses still have to trudge into open court as they have done for 200 years, and put themselves at risk?

When you see how two key witnesses recently fled the State rather than give evidence in the trial of John Gilligan, it makes one wonder if the time has not arrived to reconsider the way justice conducts its hearings.

Another big change in thinking in the last thirty years has been the introduction of anonymity for victims and witnesses, and therefore the accused, in cases involving serious sexual assault. One example of how desperate victims feel in court during cross-examination – which some have described as being like a second rape – involves the collapse of a trial in May 2001 when the victim fled from the court after the questioning proved too intense. She was consoled outside by one of the investigating gardaí who attempted to calm her down. This contact was interpreted by the accused's legal team as an attempt to pervert justice, implying that the garda was schooling her in her answers, and the case collapsed. At some point, someone in a position of leadership is going to have to recognise that justice is not just about protecting the defendant's rights.

I am used to being in court to give evidence so I know what to expect and can, to some extent, take precautions. I have developed my own kind of body language of self-preservation. This involves keeping my eyes to the ground so I will not be 'eyeballed', closing my ears as I pass defendants so as not to hear their abuse, walking at a safe distance so spit will not land on me and keeping my bag in my hand at all times. That is the essence of what court means for a witness for the prosecution – the prospect of being totally exposed to the accused.

But an ordinary citizen called to give evidence or to appear on a jury is on unfamiliar territory, both in relation to the courtroom itself and to what goes on there. During my appearances as an expert witness for the State, I frequently get the impression that jurors feel intimidated by courthouses which are very much relics of an older, grander period, and are generally very formal. For many of them it's the first time they've even been in court, let alone been central to its process. It's as if sometimes the judge and barrister seem to be speaking their own language and the only way the jury can assert themselves is to acquit.

My own belief is that the non-jury system which operates on the Continent has advantages over the method of justice here. Experts simply submit reports that the legally trained public servants then talk through. In most continental countries forensic scientists never go to court. Nor is the defence given the right to hire

– at public expense – their own expert witness to challenge the independent findings. Expert witnesses have simply commercialised the business of forensic science. Huge sums of money changing hands diverts the interest from the truth to the payment. After all, how often are you going to be retained by a client if you have a reputation of delivering evidence that the defendant doesn't want to hear?

On the Continent, nothing depends on the brilliance of the barristers. Witnesses are never put at risk by having to look a criminal in the face when testifying against them.

I remember going to Castlebar Circuit Court where a young man was charged with assaulting an old woman in a very isolated cottage. He had broken windows and doors and there was a lot of solid forensic evidence. The woman was eighty-five years old, and although partially blind and very frail, she made a very good witness. The accused had many supporters in court who were standing around in a way that seemed very deliberately intended to intimidate. And because of that, after her cross-examination the judge ordered that the old woman was to be taken home by gardaí who were to stay with her until the trial was over. At lunchtime, nobody in court was allowed to leave until the jury had made it safely to a hotel, so they could not be followed. And after I gave evidence, the judge turned to me and said I had five minutes to leave, during which time nobody else could. In other words, I had five minutes to make good my escape – that was how obvious the intimidation was in court. This is what crime-fighters are up against in this country – a judicial system in which witnesses are exposed to real risk.

* * *

In my own case, the question I was most often asked after the explosion was: 'Why were you not protected? Don't those who give witness in serious crimes get garda protection?'

I did not get full-time protection until 1982, after the explosion that almost killed me. And that was the third attempt on my life.

In *The Irish Times* report on the explosion it was stated that: 'The attempt on Dr Donovan's life is the first incident in recent years in which someone has tried to murder a servant of the State other than a member of the Garda or Army ...'

This was in fact the third attempt on my life. The first was by the IRA during the trial that followed the murder of Lord Mountbatten in 1979; the second was Martin Cahill's failed effort in December 1981.

At that time there was no Witness Protection Scheme. And even if there had been, it would not have applied to a civil servant like myself; it is principally used in cases where a former associate of a criminal has turned State's Witness, and his life is judged to be in grave danger prior to, during and sometimes after the trial. In these cases protection can extend to providing a new identity and, effectively, a new life for the witness involved.

The more 'normal' protection provided by the State on a regular basis is usually given to politicians in sensitive posts, some security personnel and diplomats. At the time of the explosion, the greatest level of protection in the State was given to Mr Jim Mitchell, the then Fine Gael Justice Minister.

In relation to myself and Martin Cahill, the thinking seemed to be that Cahill was a gouger and would never get around to injuring witnesses; that he wouldn't dare take them on. But it was always dangerous to underestimate Martin Cahill.

A further attempt on my life – the fourth – occurred in 1983 when I was giving evidence in a particularly heinous crime. Criminals had become more ruthless and there were no longer any limits about what was acceptable, or passed for 'ordinary decent' crimes. A spate of attacks on elderly people living alone in rural areas illustrated how intimidation had become the norm rather than the exception.

An isolated farmhouse in North Cork had been broken into. The house was occupied by an elderly man in his eighties and his handicapped daughter who was about fifty-five years old, who could not speak. She was tied to a chair by the raiders and indecently assaulted. Her hair was set on fire in an attempt to force her father into telling them where he hid his money. The conviction against one of the assailants was secured on the basis of forensic evidence. When I left the courthouse after presenting my evidence, my car wouldn't start. On examination, the garda driver who had been assigned to me that day discovered that somebody had attempted to tamper with my brakes but had botched the job.

In 1987 an Assistant Commissioner took the decision to remove my life protection on the basis that no attempt had been made on my life 'for some time'. I felt very exposed because of the suddenness and the unexpectedness of the withdrawal of protection. My wife and I were totally unprepared.

The problem is that when you are under protection it is because somebody wants to kill you, and this thought never leaves you. For my wife and myself our whole lives had changed, as did our behaviour, because it was no longer just us in our house; it was my wife, me and the Special Branch. Ours is the only house in our estate with an outdoor toilet for all the gardaí who have at varying times manned our door. They became like family to us and I have to say that they helped us above and beyond the call of duty. Their acts of kindness gave me faith in humanity again. For instance, they would come up with ideas to ease my discomfort – like putting a foam mat under my feet in the car to reduce the friction that sent shocks of pain up my legs. Things like that – compassion – made life easier.

My wife was herself under protection for over two months when I was giving evidence on another terrorist case in 1980. Being told by the Assistant Commissioner in charge of Security that he had reason to believe my wife would be kidnapped and killed was the hardest thing I have ever had to go through. Even then, she never once said to me: Don't give evidence.

But, just when we had adapted to full-time security and started to feel safe, the protection was removed and we had to re-learn what it was like to live as vulnerable targets again.

Since protection was withdrawn, I have only had it when working on a case that involves the security of the State.

My wife and I have had bits of paper with obscenities written on them pushed through our letterbox. More frightening than these messages is the thought that those people know where we live. You can deal with something that lasts a week, but when intimidation becomes an ongoing process, it is especially difficult. People said to me: 'Why don't you move?' But I know a garda who moved house after receiving bullets in the post from a criminal and he has never stopped moving. The other thing is that our house is specially adapted to my needs as a man with a disability. I don't think I could start all over again in a new one. And, of course, I know that if I started running away, there would be no place to stop.

PART THREE
FROM SHERLOCK HOLMES TO DNA
THE WORK OF THE FORENSIC DETECTIVE

'Detection is, or ought to be, an exact science, and should be treated in the same cold and unemotional manner.'
The Sign of Four, *Sir Arthur Conan Doyle*

'FORENSIC' IS DEFINED in the dictionary as 'used in connection with courts of law'. The word is based on the Latin *forensis* (from the word *forum*), so forensic evidence is that which is suitable for presentation in a court of law. All evidence in court will be either personal, as in an eye-witness account, or physical, as in a fingerprint. Personal evidence is always highly subjective, since ten people who witness the same incident are likely to come up with ten different versions of the event. But physical evidence is objective and remains the same for each observer.

Physical evidence can take any form. It can be as large as a house or as small as a fibre. It can be as permanent as a rock or as fleeting as a smell. Its importance is that it can establish that the suspect has been in contact with the victim or the crime. It can identify criminals and it can exonerate the innocent. And suspects confronted with physical evidence which implicates them tend to confess.

CHAPTER 5: THE AIM OF FORENSICS

THE AIM OF ALL FORENSIC SCIENCE is to first identify the evidence – such as a hair being human as against animal in origin or a white powder substance being cocaine as against flour. Next, it is crucial that the evidence be 'individualised', in other words the hair linked to the person to whom it belongs or the cocaine's origin or batch established. Individualisation is made possible by the principle that no two things in nature are exactly the same. Everyone knows this to be true of fingerprints and snowflakes, but it is also true to say that no two things are ever manufactured in exactly the same way, wear away in exactly the same way or break in exactly the same way. For instance, say a motorist collides with a cyclist and flees the scene, leaving a chip of paint from the car's body-frame on the bicycle. If the paint chip can be fitted like a jigsaw piece into the scratch mark on the suspect's car and is the same colour and made of the same components, then it can be individualised as probably having come from the car and linked to the scene.

However, absolute certainty is anathema to the scientist. Take a fibre found at the scene of a crime which is identified as being white cotton. Let us say that the material being worn by the suspect also happens to be a white cotton shirt; it still cannot be conclusively individualised as having come from the suspect since the incidence of other people wearing white cotton shirts is too high. So forensic scientists apply the rules of probability when individualising items. It is possible, using a mathematical formula, to calculate the chances of the white fibre belonging to the suspect, taking into account all factors. Putting it another way, Newcomb's rule states that, 'The probability of concurrence of all events is equal to the continued product of the probabilities of all the separate events.' Even DNA fingerprinting, which is the most accurate method ever of establishing the identity of an individual, is always calculated to the probability factor.

CHAPTER 6:
THE FICTIONAL DETECTIVE
Sherlock Holmes

BY THE AGE OF ELEVEN I was gorging myself on the great detective mysteries, especially the novels of Sherlock Holmes, written by Sir Arthur Conan Doyle.

I could not have chosen a better mentor. Conan Doyle was ahead of his time, creatively inventing what science had yet to discover. He predicted that the scene of the crime would yield scientific clues about the crime itself and also about the perpetrator. He describes Holmes's use of the magnifying glass and measuring tape, both of which became crucial in the art of scene-of-crime examination. The position of the body, its relation to various objects at the scene, all reveal something of the manner in which death occurred. And it was Holmes, after all, who first applied the infant disciplines of fingerprinting, firearm identification, serology, and document examination.

When Dr Watson and the public were introduced to Sherlock Holmes in 1887, they found him developing a chemical test for bloodstains in a hospital laboratory. Yet the specific test for the identification of human blood – the immunological precipitant test – was not invented until 1901, and the more general test, using benzidine to identify the blood of any animal source, until 1904. The precise passage from *A Study in Scarlet* is uncanny in its vision. The scene is set as Holmes adds certain chemicals to a tiny amount of blood diluted in a litre of water:

A few white crystals and then … some drops of a transparent fluid … In an instant the contents assumed a dull mahogany colour, and a brownish dust was precipitated to the bottom of the glass jar.

'I've found it. I've found it,' he shouted to my companion, running towards us with a test tube in his hand. 'I have found a reagent which is precipitated by haemoglobin and by nothing else …Why, man, it is the most practical medico-legal discovery for years. Don't you see that it gives us an infallible test for blood stains?

'… The old guaiacum test was very clumsy and uncertain. So is the microscopic examination for blood corpuscles. The latter is valueless if the stains are a few hours old. Now, this appears to act as well whether the blood is old or new. Had this test been invented, there are hundreds of men now walking the earth who would long ago have paid the penalty of their crimes … Criminal cases are continually hinging upon that one point. A man is suspected of a crime months perhaps after it has been committed. His linen or clothes are examined and brownish stains discovered upon them. Are they blood stains, or rust stains, or fruit stains, or what are they? That is a question which has puzzled many an expert and why? Because there was no reliable test. Now we have the Sherlock Holmes test, and there will no longer be any difficulty.'

By styling Holmes 'the scientific detective', Conan Doyle has been dubbed the true father of forensic science. His hero would spend the day in the lab, when he was not in the dissecting rooms. There were 'the scientific charts up on the wall, the acid-charred bench of chemicals'. Another passage hammers home the author's amazing forensic foresight:

> He whipped a tape measure and a large round magnifying glass from his pocket. With these two implements he trod noiselessly about the room, sometimes stopping, occasionally kneeling, and once lying flat upon his face. So engrossed was he with his occupation that he appeared to have forgotten our presence, for he chattered away to himself under his breath the whole time, keeping up a running fire of exclamations and little cries suggestive of encouragement and of hope. As I watched him I was irresistibly reminded of a pure-blooded, well trained foxhound as it dashes backwards and forwards through the covert, whining in its eagerness, until it comes across the lost scent. For twenty minutes or more he continued his researches, measuring with the most exact care the distance between marks which were entirely invisible to me, and occasionally applying his tape to the walls in an equally incomprehensible manner. In one place he gathered up very carefully a little pile of grey dust from the floor, and packed it away in an envelope ...

> 'They say that genius is an infinite capacity for taking pains,' he remarked with a smile. 'It's a bad definition, but it does apply to detective work.'

Conan Doyle also has his hero linking specific human hair to a particular person, long before it could be done in real life. Other explorations of the great man – the microscopic detection of copper and zinc used by counterfeiters and a litmus test that seals the fate of a suspect by revealing that a solution is acidic – all are genuine forensic techniques in use today.

He also describes the power of soil identification, the use of footprint casts and trace analysis of poison on the tip of a murderous dart.

In *The Sign of Four* Holmes distinguishes between the ashes of various tobaccos to identify 140 forms of cigar, cigarette and pipe tobacco. He also established the fact that ashes in themselves might be of evidential value, which is a key forensic concept. For example, from the ashes of a cremated body it is possible to establish whether that person was poisoned in life.

CHAPTER 7:
THE REAL-LIFE DETECTIVES

WHILE CONAN DOYLE'S SHERLOCK HOLMES was solving crimes by unheard-of methods in the fictional world, in the real world scientists and investigators were making discoveries which would have a major impact on the detection of crime and the identification of criminals.

ANTHROPOMETRY

ONE OF THESE WAS A FRENCHMAN, Alphonse Bertillon (1853–1914). Alphonse was the son of Louis Bertillon, an anthropologist who devoted much of his work to proving that each human being had unique variations in physical characteristics. Alphonse realised that this might have practical value in police work. He worked out a complicated and thorough system of identification using eleven different body measurements. He reasoned that if the physical differences of convicted criminals were taken and the data classified, repeat offenders could be apprehended more readily.

In October, 1879 Bertillon presented a report to the then Prefect of Police, Louis Andrieux, who was slow to react. But three

years later, when Andrieux had been succeeded by Jean Came-
casse, Bertillon was given the chance to try out his theories on a
pilot basis. The trial period was from December 1882 to February 1883 and his system was called Anthropometry – later to be
re-named Bertillonage. On 20 February 1883, two weeks before
his time ran out, Bertillon turned up the name of a thief called
Martin with exactly the same characteristics as a thief calling
himself Dupont. When Martin confessed to being Dupont, the
future of Bertillonage seemed assured. By the following year,
the system had identified 300 prisoners with previous convictions, earning for Bertillon the mantle of 'the father of criminal
identification'. In 1892 he was appointed director of the Bureau
of Identification of the Paris police. Before long, police departments around the world were using Bertillonage. But despite
his glorious beginnings, by the end of his career Bertillon had
been discredited by his system's fallibility.

The Two William Wests

IN 1903 A NEWLY CONVICTED PRISONER named Will West arrived
at Leavenworth Prison in the US. His measurements were
taken according to Bertillon's system. However, although his
papers indicated that he was a new prisoner, one of the clerks
had the feeling that he had measured him before. On checking
the prison files he found that he already had a file on William
West, who had the same Bertillon measurements. There was
one problem. This William West was still in prison. They were
two different men.

The men were brought together and were found to resemble
one another as if they had been twins. Their Bertillon measurements were virtually identical. But there was one way to

distinguish them: their fingerprints were unmistakeably different. This led to a re-think of the Bertillon system among police forces in the US, but in other countries, including his native France, it was still very much in vogue.

The Missing Mona Lisa and the Dreyfus Case

ON 21 AUGUST 1911, LEONARDO DA VINCI'S *MONA LISA* was stolen from the Louvre museum in Paris. The museum had recently put glass frames in front of its most treasured masterpieces in order to protect them, but the public and critics disapproved. They felt that the glass was too reflective. Louis Béraud, a painter, decided to join the debate by painting a picture of a girl fixing her hair in the reflection from the pane of glass in front of the *Mona Lisa*. However, when he went to view the painting he found it missing.

Bertillon was summoned to save the day. The plate glass and the picture frame were discovered on a staircase in the museum. Although Bertillon found a clear fingerprint on the frame, he was unable to match it. Bertillon had been an active opponent of the science of dactylography or fingerprinting, because its proponents threatened to overshadow his own system. The *Mona Lisa* was missing for two years. The thief eventually turned out to be an Italian named Vincenzo Peruggia, who had stolen the painting because he felt it rightfully belonged in the country of Leonardo da Vinci's birth – Italy. He was arrested when he tried to sell the painting to the Uffizi Gallery in Florence.

Bertillon's failure in this case severely diminished his reputation. Then an earlier case, in which his evidence had been crucial in sending a man to prison, came back to haunt him.

The Dreyfus Affair

BERTILLON WAS A WITNESS FOR THE PROSECUTION in the Dreyfus case. He had claimed that the handwriting of Alfred Dreyfus matched French military documents being leaked by a spy to the Germans in 1894. Dreyfus was an obscure captain in the French army, a Jew in a time when there was a fiercely anti-semitic climate, and the evidence was willingly believed. He was sentenced to life imprisonment on the notorious Devil's Island – a penal colony located off the coast of South America. The case became one of the most celebrated international miscarriages of justice, partly because of the intervention of the novelist Émile Zola, who published a famous denunciation of the army cover-up in a daily newspaper, under the heading 'J'accuse!'. In 1906 Dreyfus was exonerated of all charges. The culprit had been another officer, so the handwriting claims of Bertillon were disproved. The stoic captain returned to the army, was promoted and received the *Légion d'Honneur*. After this, Bertillon's system was totally discredited.

However, Bertillon did make a great contribution to forensic science in another field – photography. He insisted on photographing the bodies of victims and their relationship to significant items of evidence at the scene. He also photographed other items, recording the size, nature and extent of other physical evidence, including footprints, stains, tool-marks and points of entry and exit.

Hannibal Lecter

AND BERTILLON HAS NOT BEEN FORGOTTEN. Thomas Harris, author of *The Silence of the Lambs*, displayed a familiarity with Bertillon's chart for identifying the colour of a criminal's eyes when he used the word 'maroon' to describe the eyes of his most notorious creation, Hannibal Lecter: 'Dr Lecter's eyes are maroon and they reflect the light in pin-points of red.' The first Hannibal Lecter book, *Red Dragon,* is introduced by a quote from Bertillon: 'One can only see what one observes, and one observes only things which are already in the mind.'

CRIMINALISTICS

THE FIRST TRUE SCIENTIFIC DETECTIVE was Dr Hans Gross, an Austrian magistrate dubbed 'the father of criminalistics'. Dr Gross published the first book to apply scientific disciplines to the field of criminal investigation in 1893. The book, translated in English as *Criminal Investigation,* instructed investigators to consider the cause and effect principle when reconstructing a crime scene in a frame-by-frame analysis: 'Nothing can be known if nothing has happened,' Gross said.

In a course on the subject, Dr Gross also described how to give a *portrait parle,* or accurate description of a suspect, which is the natural forerunner of the identikit, later succeeded by the photofit. Dr Gross wrote: 'The theoretical course consists of lectures or classes in which the professor describes in exact and scientific terms the various characteristics of the forehead, the nose, the ear, the lips, the mouth, the chin, etc. The walls of the lecture room are covered with numbered life-size photographs of heads, so that when the description is finished the pupils can look around and point out heads containing the characteristics described.' The nose could be adequately described based on whether the depth of the root was small, medium or large; the profile: concave, rectilinear, convex, arched, irregular, or sinuous; the base: raised, horizontal, depressed; and the height, projection and size: small, medium or large.

Dr Gross also advocated physical evidence over witness testimony: 'The progress of criminology means less trust in witnesses and more in real proof,' he wrote. He declared fingerprinting so superior to Bertillonage that he suggested the latter should be dispensed with permanently.

EVIDENCE

THE WORK OF DR EDMOND LOCARD, a student of Bertillon's, is considered the cornerstone of forensic science. Locard's 'exchange theory' declared that when there is contact between two items there will be an exchange. In other words it recognised that when any person comes into contact with an object or another person, a cross-transfer of physical evidence occurs – at crime scenes and between items of evidence and victims. Locard went on to become director of the world's first crime laboratory in Lyons, France. He proved his theory very effectively in his investigation of the murder by strangulation of a young woman in Lyons in 1912. The woman's fiancé, Émile Gourbin, seemed to have no motive for the crime and had an alibi. Locard examined a substance under his fingernails and found it to be flakes of skin coated with a fine powder made up of precisely the same chemicals and matching the pink colour of the cosmetic powder used by the victim on her face and neck. When presented with this evidence, Gourbin made a full confession and was convicted of murder.

Locard was a disciple of Gross and Sherlock Holmes. He focused much of his attention on the 'problem of dust' or trace evidence cross-transfer. 'I must confess that if in the police laboratory of Lyons we are interested in any unusual way in this problem of dust it is because of having absorbed the ideas formed in Gross and Conan Doyle,' he said.

FINGERPRINTING

MEANWHILE, BERTILLON'S WORST FEARS were coming to pass as the new science of fingerprinting seemed capable of the kind of investigative breakthroughs which the Bertillonage system had promised, but failed, to deliver.

Fingerprinting may have been the future, but it was itself marred by internal squabbles over who in fact had discovered it. The ancient Chinese were the first to adopt fingerprints for authenticating documents, using their thumbs pressed into sealing wax by way of signature. But in the early 1860s, William Herschel, a young administrative clerk in colonial India, began to notice differences in the fingerprint signatures being used by illiterate, retired Bengali soldiers to double-claim their pensions. By requiring all claimants to register their fingerprints on both their pay book and their receipt it was possible to check them against each other for fraud. After many more years he was able to prove that fingerprints do not change with age (in fact they stay the same from the sixth month of gestation in the womb until death).

The Man Who Tried to Remove His Fingerprints

THERE IS A NOTED CASE from about twenty years ago of an American career criminal who tried to slice off his own fingertips. He then created open wounds on the underside of his arms, intending to graft smooth skin from his arms onto the tips of his fingers. Despite his barbarism, his fingertips grew back. There are also recorded cases of criminals dipping their fingers in caustic solutions, which is effective in some instances.

Around the same time as Herschel was making his breakthrough, one Dr Henry Faulds, a Scottish physiologist and medical missionary attached to the Tsuki Hospital in Tokyo, had made a similar discovery about the potential of fingerprinting in the fight against crime. In the summer of 1879, a Tokyo thief who made his escape over a newly-painted wall, left behind a dirty handprint. Comparing this print with that of the suspect, Faulds concluded it was the same man. When confronted with the evidence, the thief confessed to the crime. Faulds communicated his discovery to *Nature*, the London magazine for gentlemen scientists: 'When bloody finger marks or impressions on clay, glass, etc. exist, they may lead to the scientific identification of criminals ... There can be no doubt as to the advance of having, besides their photographs, a naturecopy of the forever unchangeable finger furrows of important criminals' (October 1880). William Herschel arrived back in England at the time of publication of the article and there followed an acrimonious exchange of letters as to who had been first to make the breakthrough.

But it is to another British man, Sir Francis Galton, that credit generally goes for making the first definitive study of the subject. He developed a method of classification, detailed in *Finger Prints*, published in 1892, in which he established the first statistical proof of the uniqueness of the prints.

Galton observed basic recurring shapes and configurations of triangles and deltas, and discerned four basic patterns. But Galton's place in history was also undermined, in his case by his attempts in another sphere – he tried to prove statistically the number of times prayers worked!

In 1898, in *The Classification and Uses of Finger Prints*, the Inspector General of the Bengal police laid down five discernible patterns which are still in use today: Arches, Tented Arches, Radial Loops, Ulna Loops and Whorls. His thesis earned him the post of head of Scotland Yard's new Fingerprint branch.

The Lisdoonvarna 'Glove of Flesh'

ALMOST A HUNDRED YEARS LATER, Ireland also contributed to the research on the remarkably enduring nature of fingerprints when arsonists set fire to the Belvue Hotel in Lisdoonvarna, County Clare, in 1978. Three criminals laced the property with petrol and one struck a match. A ball of flame rolled through the hotel, blackening everything, including the crooks. One died almost immediately from his injuries, and another, who had worn gloves so as not to leave evidence of his involvement, experienced a sudden flash of heat in his hand. The glove had caused a pressure build-up resulting in the outer layer of flesh expanding away from his hand. Gardaí recovered the glove and inside it an inner glove of flesh from which we were able to take a set of five prints. A year later, following his full recovery, the arsonist was invited to give a set of prints. The comparison with the glove of flesh was positive and proved that fingerprint patterns are not diminished even in the most extreme conditions. This shows the remarkable ability of the DNA molecule in the body; not only does it retain the detail of the fingerprints but it can regrow five full prints that are exact replicas of the originals.

BALLISTICS

THE HISTORY OF BALLISTICS GOES BACK TO 1889 when the French professor, Alexandre Lacassagne, announced his conviction that the marks on a bullet recovered from a victim could be matched with the gun which had fired the shot, if the gun could be found. As a qualified surgeon, he used his experience on the field in North Africa to examine gunshot wounds, and at the end of his service he brought his findings together in the 1878 publication, *Précis de Medecine*. In 1880 he took the newly-founded Chair in Forensic Medicine at the University of Lyons. The maxim which he taught his students was: 'One must know how to doubt.' Lacassagne was also the first to attempt to study the relationship between the patterns made by bloodstains in an attack.

The Deadly Ballad

THE FIRST RECORDED CASE of linking a gunshot wound to the person who inflicted it occurred in 1794 in Lancashire, England. Gunpowder had been poured down the barrel of a single-shot, flintlock gun holding a round lead bullet; the charge was then packed home with a ramrod which had a wad of paper at its tip. Part of the paper, which contained a street ballad, tore in the gun barrel. When the shot was fired, it carried the paper wadding into the wound. On the suspect was found the remaining piece of the ballad, which matched perfectly.

But it was the American army doctor, Colonel Calvin Goddard, who laid the groundwork for the individualisation of weapons by refining the process of comparing markings on a bullet from a shooting victim with those on one test-fired for forensic examination. Goddard developed the comparison microscope, which allows two samples to be observed alongside each other so that likeness and differences are immediately discernible.

A ballistics expert can usually link the shape and design of a cartridge to a particular type of gun. Retrieving spent cartridges from the scene of a crime and comparing them with controlled shots fired from a suspect's weapon has nothing to do with ballistics, but everything to do with forensic techniques of examining, comparing and identifying evidence. The pulling of the trigger, the fall of the hammer and the explosion of the priming mixture will leave markings on the shell case which are distinct to every weapon. The trajectory of the shot will be affected by the downward pull of gravity, the speed of the flight, the yaw factor – the tendency of the bullet to wobble as it first leaves the barrel – the penetration and the ricochet, or where a bullet changes direction as it hits an object at an extreme angle. It is also possible to match a bullet with a particular gun barrel. The inside of a gun barrel is 'rifled', ie, grooves are cut into it which cause a bullet to spin as it is propelled through the barrel; the bullet will pick up any flaws in the grooves or imperfections due to wear and tear, resulting in a match between the markings on the bullet and this particular gun. When a firearm is discharged, gunpowder, nitrates, lead, barium and other chemicals will be spewed onto the target. These patterns can be analysed to estimate distance.

SEROLOGY – the Study of Blood

SINCE 1901 IT HAS BEEN POSSIBLE to link a person to a crime scene by analysing their blood. Dr Karl Landsteiner, working in the pathology department at the University of Turin, was the medic who discovered that blood can be classified into different categories, depending on the presence or absence of different antigens, which produce the antibodies that fight disease.

He classified the blood groups as A, B, AB and O. The average percentage breakdown for the various blood groups is: Group A, 42% of the population; B, 9%; AB, 3% and O, 46%.

In a further advance in 1915, Leon Lattes, a professor at the Institute of Forensic Medicine, developed an application of Landsteiner's discovery to dried blood. This was a crucial step for crime scene detectives, since blood is often scrubbed away so it is invisible to the naked eye but can still be detected under an ultra-violet beam when it appears as a brownish stain.

The ability to classify blood into a category meant that if traces of blood belonging to group O were found on a murder suspect's clothing, and he belonged to group A, the blood could not have been the suspect's own. But if the victim's blood group was O then that blood could – but only could – have come from him.

In the spring of 2001 my own Lab held a training course for staff, updating them about the latest pattern analysis and encouraging them to do their own research on chunks of pork by injecting blood under the surface. From the shape of a stain you can also tell the distance which blood has travelled, enabling detectives to place the body in the crime scene at different stages of the attack to build up an accurate reconstruction. Depending on the orientation of a blob, splashes will reveal the direction they have travelled and spurts are a sign that the body was alive at the time of a sudden impact, since the heart is a pump-like device. This fact is important when distinguishing whether the scene where blood has been found was used for a murder or dismemberment, or both. Pools of blood show the victim has lain dead for some time and smears are an indication of a victim having thrashed against the assailant before death.

Trails or drops show that a body has been dragged from one location to another. The most obvious use to gardaí would be when someone who denies causing another's death is found to be bloodstained and claims that the blood was transferred when they attempted to aid the deceased. But if the blood spatters on the suspect are round or pear-shaped, then that person was near the body when it began to spurt blood.

The Trial without a Body

THE CASE OF JACK EVANS – one of the few that went to trial without a body being recovered – illustrates the value of being able to identify dried bloodstains. Jack Evans, originally from New Zealand, was living in Dunbittern, outside Bantry, County Cork, where he did some work as a gunsmith. In July 1988 a local man who had given Evans his gun to be repaired, went back to collect it and found nobody at the house. He called several more times, with no result. Soon it became obvious that Evans was no longer in the neighbourhood. At this point the man went to Bantry Garda Station and reported the loss of his gun and the seeming disappearance of Evans. Gardaí went to Evans's house and what they found there made them suspicious. They preserved the scene and sent for the technical bureau who came down to investigate.

One of the rooms in the house had been re-painted, but, using their ultra-violet technology, the forensics people were able to determine that under the paint there was extensive bloodstaining. Other findings suggested that someone, most likely the missing Jack Evans, had been killed in the room.

There was a history to the property in which Evans lived which suggested who might have been involved in his disappearance. Wilhelm Diemling, possibly an Austrian, had lived in the cottage and had set up a joinery in an adjacent building. In order to raise money to start the business he had put his house up as collateral. When the joinery business went bust the bank foreclosed on the house. At the time Jack Evans was a tenant in part of the house, and, not wanting to be involved in an eviction, the bank let Evans buy the house for very little – thought to be around £9,000. However, the assumption locally was that, in fact, Diemling had put up most of the purchase money for Evans so that he, Diemling, would not lose the house. But, when the house was bought and legally in Evans's name, he decided to hold onto it.

On the weekend of Evans's disappearance, Wilhelm Diemling, who had been living in England, was seen back in the Bantry area in a blue Volkswagen pick-up truck. He was accompanied by another man, from Bracknell in England.

It is thought that Diemling went to see Evans on the Friday, and between Friday and Sunday, tortured and beat Evans until he eventually died. The body was then cut up and burned. Diemling returned to England.

An extradition warrant was issued for Diemling and he was brought back to Ireland and put on trial, charged with the false imprisonment and murder of Jack Evans. Sometime in 1990 he was convicted on both charges and went to prison. However, he continued to appeal the murder conviction and, after several appeals, the State decided that he was entitled to a re-trial. However, the State never proceeded with the re-trial and he was released, having served seven years on the charge of false imprisonment of Jack Evans.

Someone who had spoken to Diemling in Cork reported him

as saying that Evans's body would never be found, and it wasn't. However, the gardaí had reason to believe that what remained of the body had been put in a barrel and dumped over the bridge at Snave, near Ballylickey, County Cork, but as the body was not found, this could not be proven.

DNA: GENETIC FINGERPRINTING

WHILE BLOOD GROUPING NARROWED THE POSSIBILITIES for investigators, certainty came with the discovery of DNA or deoxyribonucleic acid – a self-replicating material which is present in nearly all living organisms, and is the carrier of genetic information. DNA is often called the building block of life.

The DNA molecule was identified as early as 1911 as that which carried genetic information. By the 1950s the DNA structure was discovered by two British scientists, James Watson and Francis Crick. But it was not until 1984 that a team in Leicester University, working under geneticist Dr Alec Jeffreys, discovered that this double helix structure is unique to each individual. They also developed a way of isolating the DNA code from body fluids or tissues and x-raying the fragments. The result coined the term 'genetic fingerprinting', which refers to the barcode-like pattern of stripes that is different in every individual.

Genetic fingerprinting revolutionised forensic serology and in 1986 its potential in the fight against crime was shown in the first murder case where it was used.

Lynda Mann and Dawn Ashworth –
The First Mass DNA Screening

IN 1983 FIFTEEN-YEAR-OLD LYNDA MANN was raped and strangled on a secluded footpath in the village of Narborough in
Leicestershire, leading detectives to believe the murderer was a
local man who knew the area well. But the investigation went
nowhere. Nearly three years later, a second fifteen-year-old,
Dawn Ashworth, was raped and murdered on another quiet
path in nearby Enderby. The West Midlands police asked Dr
Jeffreys to help in the investigation. They announced that they
were about to take 'a revolutionary step', which involved the
first mass DNA screening of males living in the nearby Leicestershire villages. 'Blood buses' were driven to housing estates
and factories. It was a massively expensive experiment which
threatened to be extremely embarrassing when it ruled out the
prime suspect and failed to throw up an alternative. In fact, the
killer, Colin Pitchfork, had evaded the screening by persuading
a friend to impersonate him and give a blood sample on his
behalf. He had told his friend that he could not give blood
because he had already 'helped out' someone else – a friend
with a police record for flashing. By 1987, with no result to
show for its efforts, it looked as though the investigating team
would be unable to justify any more funding. Then Pitchfork's
employer – a manager in a bakery – heard workers gossiping
about the fact that Pitchfork had got someone to give a sample
for him. The bakery manager told the police who lost no time in
arriving on Pitchfork's doorstep and taking a sample. This time
the DNA matched that found in the semen left in the bodies of
the dead girls. The police had their man, and it was all thanks to
DNA.

Advances in DNA technology are developing all the time. You don't even need a body anymore, just remains. Mitochondrial DNA extracted from bones will reveal the same genetic make-up as found in blood cells and in other bodily fluids.

James Hanratty & the A6 Murder

ONE OF THE EFFECTS OF THESE ADVANCES is to allow investigators to revisit old cases, which were either unsolved or where there is reason to doubt the verdict. Twenty-five-year-old James Hanratty went to the gallows in Britain on 4 April 1962 protesting his innocence. Hanratty was charged with the murder of Michael Gregsten at a layby on the A6 near Bedford in August 1961. Valerie Storie, Gregsten's lover, had also been raped and shot five times before their attacker fled, leaving her for dead. Valerie Storie survived but was paralysed. James Hanratty's conviction was based almost solely on the discovery of two .38 cartridge cases from the murder weapon in the hotel room where he stayed the night before, using the alias James Ryan. A campaign to clear Hanratty's name began almost immediately after the hanging and gathered momentum down through the years. On 22 March 2001 James Hanratty's remains were exhumed from Carpenders Park cemetery in Bushey, Hertfordshire, so that a DNA sample could be taken for analysis. On 4 April 2001 the *Guardian* newspaper reported: 'Sources at Scotland Yard confirmed that the tests conducted by the forensic science service ... were positive, and that there was a "one in 100m chance" that the DNA came from another person. The results concluded that his DNA "perfectly matches" strands found on the victim's clothes.

The results will be central to the upcoming appeal hearing.

ODONTOLOGY

FORENSIC ODONTOLOGY IS THE SCIENTIFIC APPLICATION of dentistry to legal matters and specialists in the science learn how to identify an individual through the teeth. A person's dental records will reveal jaw structure, fillings, extractions and other repairs carried out during their lifetime that can be used for comparison after they are dead – teeth are the longest-enduring part of the body, *post mortem*. The age of a victim can also be estimated with considerable accuracy up to twenty-five years by the stage of growth of the teeth.

The Notorious Ted Bundy

BITEMARKS CAN ALSO BE COMPARED TO A SUSPECT'S TEETH. Notorious serial killer Ted Bundy, who carried out a reign of terror in the US during the 1970s, made a fatal mistake when he left bite marks on the buttocks of one of his victims, Lisa Levy. At his trial, odontologist Dr Richard Souviron described to the jury the indentations left by the bitemarks and showed photographs of Bundy's teeth, demonstrating that the marks made a perfect match. These photos were the biggest piece of evidence in the trial and the jury had no doubts. They returned a verdict of guilty, and Bundy was executed on 24 June 1989. While in prison awaiting execution he confessed to the murders of twenty-eight young women, but many are convinced that the numbers were far higher.

CRIMINAL PROFILING

THE DEDUCTIVE REASONING OF SHERLOCK HOLMES pre-empted the development of forensic psychology, which today assesses the mindset of the perpetrator from the manner in which the crimes were committed and the devastation they have left behind.

The criterion on which it is based is remarkably sound due to the pioneering work of Dr James Brussel in the United States in 1957. He claimed that since a psychiatrist can study a person and predict their behaviour patterns in the future, it was possible to invert the theory and by studying someone's past actions and responses to come up with a picture or profile of the type of person likely to be responsible for these actions.

The Mad Bomber

IN 1957 BRUSSEL STUDIED THE CRIMES OF New York's 'Mad Bomber' who for sixteen years had used explosives to wage a war of terror against the Consolidated Edison Company. Dr Brussel's profile of the man police should be looking for stated: 'Single man between forty and fifty years old, introvert. Unsocial but not anti-social. Skilled mechanic. Cunning. Neat with tools. Egotistical of mechanical skill. Contemptuous of other people. Resentful of criticism of his work but probably conceals resentment. Moral. Honest. Not interested in women. High school graduate. Expert in civil or military ordnance. Religious. Might flare up violently at work when criticised. Possible motive: discharge or reprimand. Feels superior to critics. Resentment keeps growing. Present or former Consolidated Edison worker. Probably case of progressive paranoia.' The profile led police straight to the door of George Metsky, a disgruntled ex-Edison Company employee, just as Dr Brussel had predicted.

The Boston Strangler

IN 1964 DR BRUSSEL HAD ANOTHER HIT when he stated that 'The Boston Strangler', who sexually assaulted and killed eleven women between 1962 and 1963 was a paranoid schizophrenic, around thirty years of age, of average height but strongly built, of Spanish or Italian extraction, with a head of thick dark hair, but clean-shaven. Albert de Salvo, who was eventually convicted of the killings, matched this description perfectly.

These successes silenced the sceptics, and when the increasing numbers of serial killers led to palpable public alarm, the FBI set up the Behavioural Science Unit at Quantico in Virginia. By 1985 the FBI Academy had introduced the Violent Criminal Apprehension Programme (Vi-Cap), which identifies common patterns in murders through comparing reports from all over the United States – attempting to establish links. In Britain, the Home Office Enquiry System (or HOLMES, after the fictional detective) began to compile similar information following the lack of co-ordination in the tracking down of the Yorkshire Ripper, Peter Sutcliffe.

The Railway Rapist

THE FIRST KILLER TO BE IDENTIFIED in Britain by the use of Psychological Offender Profiling (POP) was John Duffy, aka 'the Railway Rapist'. Between 1982 and 1986 he and an accomplice murdered three women and were responsible for over twenty rapes, using London's Rail and Tube network to stalk their victims.

Professor David Canter, an expert in behavioural science and professor of applied psychology at Surrey University, was brought in on the case. He made deductions that the killer lived in the Kilburn-Cricklewood area of northwest London, was unhappily married and childless. His profile was accurate in thirteen of its seventeen points.

John Duffy, an unemployed carpenter from Kilburn, was arrested and charged with the murder of nineteen-year-old Alison Day on 23 December 1985 and the murder of fifteen-year-old Dutch girl Maartje Tamboezen on 17 April 1986.

Following Duffy's capture, Professor Canter explained: 'A criminal leaves evidence of his personality through his actions in relation to a crime. Any person's behaviour exhibits characteristics unique to that person, as well as patterns and consistencies which are typical of the sub-group to which he or she belongs.'

Duffy was jailed for life in 1988 for two murders, five rapes and a sex assault. After some time in prison Duffy began to talk and identified his accomplice, David Mulcahy. In February, 2001 Mulcahy was given three life sentences for the rape and murder of three women and for the rape of a further seven women. Duffy himself was charged with a further seventeen rapes and received an additional twelve-year jail sentence.

Profilers are now routinely engaged at major crime scenes to examine the devastation left behind and to draw conclusions about the perpetrator. Their findings can guide investigation teams as to the age group, gender, marital status, race, occupation, criminal record, sexual preferences etc. of the criminal they are looking for.

But long before forensic profiling became a science I would have subscribed to its powers. By the end of his career, it was clear to me, for instance, that Martin Cahill's behavioural patterns had made him a walking cliché in profiling terms.

CHAPTER 8:
SCIENCE ON THE FRINGES
Head Shapes and Handwriting

NATURALLY ENOUGH, SOME SCIENCES have given birth to pseudo sciences and forensic science is no exception.

The ancient Jews were the first to recognise that each individual's handwriting varied. Identification is based on analysis of form, line quality and arrangement. The science inspired a pseudo science called graphology, which offers to analyse a personality through the handwriting and has no evidential basis whatsoever.

The FBI lab have taken a more useful approach. The organisation has collected an archive of questioned documents which include anonymous letters, fraudulent cheques, bank robbery notes. What is known as the Forensic Information System for Handwriting (FISH) permits forensic document experts to scan ransom letters or threatening correspondence and throw up probable hits. Techniques for examining questioned documents include macroscopy – the study of things with the naked eye – and microscopy.

The Hitler Diaries

IN 1983 THE GERMAN MAGAZINE *STERN* believed it had acquired the rights to the diaries of Adolf Hitler, for which it had paid about 10 million marks. It announced its coup as 'the journalistic scoop of the post World War II period'. The story was that the volumes of handwritten text had been smuggled out of Berlin in the dying days of the war but the plane carrying them had crashed and the documents had come into the possession of a collector of Nazi documentation. *Stern* paid the money to a mysterious Dr Fischer, who was supposedly smuggling the diaries in from East Germany in pianos.

The handwriting in the diaries was checked by Max Frei-Sultzer, former head of the Zurich police forensic science department, by a specialist in document verification from South Carolina, and by a German police documents expert. All compared the diary handwriting to an existing sample of Hitler's handwriting and declared the diaries authentic. In fact, they had been forged by a small-time criminal named Konrad Kujau, who, incidentally, had also forged the 'genuine sample' against which the diaries were checked, so the handwriting was definitely the same – just not Hitler's!

When the testing moved from the handwriting to the ink and paper used in the diaries, all was revealed. Forensic tests found that the paper contained a whitening agent that was first introduced in 1954, the threads attaching the seals to the volumes contained viscose and polyester – also developed after the Second World War. None of the different types of inks existed when the diaries were supposed to have been written and tests to see how long the ink had been present on the paper revealed that they had been written less than a year previously.

PHRENOLOGY

IN 1796 A VIENNESE PHYSICIAN, Dr Franz Joseph Gall, introduced the world to Phrenology. He said the shape of the brain corresponded to a person's overall personality. An assessment could be made by feeling bumps on the cranium. These, he claimed, demonstrated seven propensities, depending on where they were located, and indicated domesticity, selfishness, vanity, morality, self-perfecting, intellectual and reflective tendencies. Ironically, many psychoanalysts today attribute incidents of violence in adults to head injuries causing neurological damage, which can be tested by routine co-ordination tasks. So there may have been some truth in it!

The idea of people 'born' to be criminals intensified with the publication of Charles Darwin's *On the Origin of Species by Means of Natural Selection* in 1859. Darwin's theory of evolution and eugenics argued for a natural, not divine, production of genetically perfect offspring. Within a century, his logic would be taken to the most heinous conclusions by the medical experiments of SS Captain Josef Mengele in pursuit of the Nazi ideal of an Aryan race.

It was a contemporary of Darwin's, an Italian named Cesare Lombroso, who claimed in 1876 that he had studied 7,000 criminals in an asylum in Pesaro and had found the savage traits they had in common were large jaws, high cheekbones, square ears, and long arms. Lombroso was a prison surgeon in Toulon who published his findings under the title *L'Uomo Delinquente* (Criminal Man), which argued that plaster casts of his patients' heads demonstrated the 'degenerate' features of the skull.

In the early nineteenth century a Parisian arch-criminal turned policeman, Eugene Vidocq, developed this theory to make a real contribution to forensic science when he encouraged his officers to visit the jails to familiarise themselves with the faces of felons so that if they re-offended they would be recognised. By his retirement in the 1830s Vidocq had organised the first documentary records of the descriptions of these criminals.

Even in the twentieth century, criminologists have allowed fantastical theory to masquerade as science. In the United States, the *Gluecks* believed that the testicles of criminals differed from those of honest-living citizens!

CHAPTER 9:
GETTING AWAY WITH MURDER

ALL IN ALL, THE COMBINED DISCIPLINES of the forensic sciences make it possible to untangle lies. But, as forensic scientists and investigators become more knowledgeable and their skills more refined, so also there are criminals who are using their knowledge of forensics to try to escape the long arm of the law.

The DIY Dentist

In 1976 in England, a serial killer called Trevor Joseph Hardy, who was found to be 'mad not bad', ie, guilty but insane, had the capacity to realise that if he ground his teeth into a different shape with a metal file, he could not be linked to the bitemarks in his victims' breasts.

The Case of Dr Buck Ruxton

IN 1935, AN ENGLISH GP, DR BUCK RUXTON attempted to use his medical expertise to prevent any evidence linking him back to the murder of his wife, Isabella. When his maid, Mary Jane Rogerson, caught him in the act, the GP murdered her too, so that there would be no witness. He dismembered the bodies and attempted to remove all identifying features. Mary Jane suffered from a squint, so the eyes were removed and destroyed. Isabella had a prominent nose and teeth and these characteristics were removed. The skin over an appendix scar had also been removed, as had a birthmark. Her fingertips were sliced off.

On 29 September 1935 a woman crossing a bridge over a stream near the town of Moffat, in Scotland, saw a human arm on the bank. Police put bloodhounds on the trail and in all seventy pieces of the two bodies were collected, some wrapped in newspaper, some in cloth. The Edinburgh University Forensic Science Department received the most substantial parts of the find, including two heads. There were two upper arms and four pieces of flesh wrapped in a blouse; two legs from which most of the flesh had been stripped and nine pieces of unidentifiable flesh wrapped in a pillowcase; a cotton sheet containing seventeen pieces of flesh and another cotton sheet containing a human trunk.

The first breakthrough was that the newspaper, *The Sunday Graphic* of 15 September 1935, in which some body parts were wrapped, was part of a local edition distributed only in Morecambe and the nearby city of Lancaster. Police were meanwhile checking all missing persons' records and discovered a write-up in Glasgow's *Daily Record* about the disappearance of a young housemaid, Mary Jane Rogerson. She had been reported missing by her employer, a Lancaster doctor named Buck Ruxton, on 14 September. Ruxton's common-law wife, Isabella Van Ess, had disappeared at the same time. Clothes in which one bundle of body parts had been wrapped were identified by a family friend as belonging to Isabella. Police discovered that Dr Ruxton had arranged for his children to stay with friends on the night of 14 September and had let the help off early. After the murders he visited one of his patients – a charlady – and asked her to help him clean up the surgery. The woman told how the carpets of the stairs and hall were blood-soaked, of fires lit by Ruxton to burn clothes and of how he sprayed the house with a cologne to try and disguise a noxious smell.

Friends provided police with a motive, claiming that the relationship between the doctor and Isabella had always been stormy and that Ruxton was violent. He had got it into his head that his common-law wife was having an affair and killed her when she arrived home late.

Meanwhile the forensic team were performing minor miracles. Although the bodies were hideously dismembered, the killer obviously had anatomical knowledge because of the way the bodies were cut at the joints. Photographs of the recovered heads were overlaid with photographs of the victims taken when alive to reveal which woman was which. The tongue in Mary Rogerson's head was severely swollen – a sign that she had been strangled – and in Isabella's case the hyoid bone in the throat was damaged, indicating the same type of death.

Dr Alexander Mearns in the Institute of Hygiene at Edinburgh University was able, by identifying the life cycle of the maggots which had infested the body parts, to claim that these deaths had occurred at the same time as the two women had disappeared.

Despite all his efforts to evade prosecution, Dr Buck Ruxton faced the hangman at Strangeways Prison in Manchester on 12 May 1936.

Marilyn Rynn

ANOTHER, MORE RECENT CASE IN IRELAND which highlights the increasing awareness of forensics among criminals is that of Marilyn Rynn, the civil servant raped and strangled after getting the Nitelink bus home to Blanchardstown, Co Dublin, after her office Christmas party on 21 December 1995. Following the discovery of her body, the gardaí undertook the first mass screening programme for DNA ever used in this country. They asked men in the area to give blood and the Lab analysed the DNA samples for comparison to that found in her body. Among those who complied with the request was Marilyn's killer. David Lawlor willingly gave a blood sample because he had researched forensics on the Internet and discovered that semen will last in a woman's body for no longer than six days; then it will disintegrate. It was twelve days before Marilyn's body was found. Lawlor assumed he was safe.

But in those twelve days, the weather was cold but extremely calm, with little rain and little frost. We had found enough semen – a tiny quantity; you could hardly trace it – but we found it. And it matched David Lawlor's DNA sample. Lawlor lived only 400 yards away from where the body was dumped. His wife and his mother-in-law were in the house on the night Marilyn disappeared and they remembered him coming in and putting his clothing into the washing machine; something he had never done before. Lawlor also knew that detergents would destroy any traces of his victim's blood on his clothing.

Another attempt to thwart justice had been foiled.

Harold Shipman – Doctor Jekyll of Hyde

DOCTOR HAROLD SHIPMAN WAS a very popular GP. His surgery at Market Street in Hyde in Greater Manchester was open six days a week and the waiting room was usually full. He had a list of 3,100 patients, but he was doing his best to reduce that number. On 1 February 2000 Harold Shipman was convicted of the murder of fifteen of his patients. In all, detectives have investigated the deaths of 130 of the doctor's former patients and the feeling is that while the exact number of his victims may never be known, it could amount to over two hundred.

Doctor Shipman's chosen murder weapon was morphine, a substance that would be difficult for the lay person to obtain legally but was readily available to a doctor, particularly one who had many elderly patients requiring pain relief. In fact, it was not the first time the doctor had used drugs for his own ends – he was a convicted drug addict. In the mid 1970s, when he was a young GP in West Yorkshire, Harold Shipman had become addicted to pethedine. He prescribed the medicine for patients but kept it for himself, a method he was to use later to secure the morphine he needed for his killing spree. In the 1970s when his addiction came to light, he was fined, reprimanded and received counselling, but was not struck off the Medical Register.

In 1977 Shipman joined a medical practice in Hyde and built up a reputation as an efficient, conscientious doctor, respected by his colleagues and patients. In 1993 he set up his own practice in Market Street.

Three years later, in March 1995, he killed eighty-one-year-old widow Marie West. Other murders followed, with increasing frequency: Irene Turner, aged sixty-seven, in 1996, Lizzie

Adams (77) in February 1997, Jean Lilley (59) in April 1997, Ivy Lomas (63) in May 1997. There were four more murders in 1997 and six in 1998, the last being Kathleen Grundy. All the victims were women and all except one were either widowed or single. Doctor Shipman had visited each patient on the day she died. The death certificates, made out by Shipman as the attending GP, gave the cause of death as 'coronary thrombosis', 'circulatory failure', 'stroke' or 'ischaemic heart disease'.

The death rate did not go unnoticed. Locals joked about 'Doctor Death', and there had been an inquiry into the GP's high death rate, but it was abandoned two months before Shipman killed Winifred Mellor (73) in May 1998. Mrs Mellor's death came as a complete shock to her family. They had no idea that their mother had been suffering from angina, as Doctor Shipman now informed them. They could not understand why she had never mentioned it.

A police computer expert was able to show that Shipman, afer killing Mrs Mellor, had rushed back to his computer and made additions to her medical history to show that she had a long-time history of angina. But the computer, while inserting the entries into the back records as intended, also kept a memory of the date on which the entries were *actually* made.

Kathleen Grundy was Shipman's last victim. She was killed in June 1998 and her will immediately caused alarm bells to ring. Harold Shipman was named as the sole beneficiary of her estate. But the will was a blatant forgery. Signatures had been forged and letters accompanying the will had all been typed on Dr Shipman's *Brother* typewriter. On 7 September 1998 Harold Shipman was arrested and charged with the murder of Kathleen Grundy. With suspicions heightened and families raising queries about their relatives, the investigation widened, with devastating results.

Twelve of Doctor Shipman's former patients were exhumed and traces of morphine were discovered. Julie Evans, the forensic scientist who analysed the levels of morphine found, told the trial that 'a substantial amount' of the drug was found in samples taken from the thigh and liver of Kathleen Grundy. Samples from eight other bodies also revealed morphine. Many of Doctor Shipman's other patients had been cremated.

The defence barrister told the court that the case against Shipman relied on toxicology. And the jury believed the findings. After a trial lasting fifty-seven days at Preston Crown Court, Harold Shipman was given fifteen life sentences.

The Manchester coroner, John Pollard, who knew and had worked with Shipman, said, 'I think he simply enjoyed viewing the process of dying and enjoyed the feeling of control over life and death, literally over life and death.'

After the murder conviction, Winifred Mellor's daughter said, 'I am sick of the whole notion that doctors are untouchables. Who else has this tremendous protection of reputation?'

And who else could find it so easy, for so long, to get away with murder?

PART FOUR
FORENSICS IN IRELAND

*'Give me problems, give me work, give me
the most abstruse cryptogram, or the most
intricate analysis, and I am in my own
proper atmosphere.'*
The Sign of Four, *Sir Arthur Conan Doyle*

CHAPTER 10: SETTING UP THE FORENSIC SCIENCE LABORATORY

ON 1 DECEMBER 1975 I WAS APPOINTED the first forensic scientist ever recruited by the State.

You have to understand that in those days the sceptics of forensic science outnumbered the believers. Forensics was still a new science and at that stage there were doubts as to whether it would be acceptable in the courts and how effective it would be at all.

It was only after numerous submissions to the Department of Justice from the Garda Síochána outlining just what scientists could do if they worked alongside the gardaí, that a sub-committee was established under the National Science Council to examine the issue. In 1972 the sub-committee recommended that the Garda Síochána needed a Forensic Science Laboratory to investigate the scientific aspects of crime. They said it should begin with eight staff and whatever accommodation and funding was necessary, and grow to thirty persons by 1980. The potential of science in the fight against crime was explained to the Government and after many months of humming and hawing, the recommendations were eventually sanctioned by the Department of Finance (although the recommended pro-gressive increase in personnel did not happen).

When I was appointed, I was told by the Department of Justice that there would never be any money for staff or for equipment and that they had a 'loan of a desk' for me in the Institute for Industrial Research and Standards office in Glasnevin. I was expected to analyse explosives and human organs and suchlike in an office where three other people were working at desks! Specimens were to go unprotected even by basic equipment like a fridge.

There was already in existence an institution known as the State Laboratory, which had been founded by law, and where I had worked from 1971. But the State Lab was, in reality, a Customs and Excise laboratory. As it fell under the aegis of the Department of Finance, its sole function was to collect money, in other words to keep the government afloat. For instance, when the government decided to tax alcohol, putting x percent on spirits and beers, it was the State Lab's function to measure the alcohol content of the drink in order to fix the levy. You pay far more tax on a glass of whiskey, for example, than you would on a glass of stout. There were tests for the amount of moisture in tobacco and textiles used in clothing, particularly after Ireland joined the European Community. The Brussels Tariff Code required member states to charge equal amounts of tax based on the composition of each material. Animal feeds had to be analysed, fertilisers measured to make sure they had the right amounts of nitrogen, phosphorous and potassium, and test results on fuel returned to customs officers who routinely checked the tanks of lorries to make sure they were not using duty-rebated diesel (dyed red to distinguish it from ordinary diesel) which farmers and sailors are allowed use but drivers are not.

Another problem was that over the years the State Laboratory had taken on a lot of things that were not really their responsibility, simply because there was nobody else to do them. I wanted to set up clear divisions and let everyone know that criminal matters were now the remit of the new Forensic Science Lab. But as there are forensic science disciplines for every complexity of the human body, this meant getting more staff and expanding the laboratory quite considerably.

Fortunately, the Garda Commissioner, Ned Garvey, was on my side and encouraged me to lobby for facilities. After several months as the State's first forensic scientist, I managed to convince my superiors that dead men do tell tales. That is their revenge – to reveal how they were killed and by whom. I was able now to insist on the other people being moved out of the office and on having the windows nailed up, and the doors secured with special locks. The Lab, if you like, was finally born.

But, of course, a science is effective only when it is applied correctly and consistently. The Garda Siochána have been outstanding in embracing the potential of the new tool at their disposal. Not long after the Lab was finalised a study was made of the application of forensic science by international police forces. This proved that the Garda Siochána used forensics as much as the top British and US police forces. In particular, I have to single out a number of gardaí who were to the forefront in championing the use of forensics in criminal investigations: Chief Superintendents Dan Murphy and John Courtney of the

Murder Squad, Inspector Ned Ryan, and Deputy Commissioner Noel Conroy. Without their efforts and the continuing efforts of all gardaí, many criminals would have slipped through the net and never been brought to justice for their crimes.

CHAPTER 11:
DEVELOPING TECHNIQUES AND
TACKLING CASES

I SET ABOUT GETTING HELP AND IN 1976 NOEL TRENCH, who had been my assistant in the State Lab, joined the Forensic Lab, along with a clerical assistant, Florence Bell. Noel was from Hollywood, County Mayo, and was extremely efficient, specialising in toxicology and the analysis of alcohol. Noel died suddenly in 1989 and his death was a huge loss. In February 1977, the scientist Dr Tim Creedon joined the Lab as a biologist, specifically to work on sex offences and murders by grouping blood and analaysing semen. In June he was joined by his technician, Judy Price who is still in the lab. They developed the Sexual Assault Kit which all Garda Stations now keep. It means that if someone alleges rape, or if a body is found, gardaí can use the tools in the kit to bring vital evidence back to the Lab for immediate testing. The kit contains cotton buds for semen and blood swabs, combs to take pubic hair samples, little metal picks used to take scrapings from the nails (since victims often claw their attackers), and vials to contain any evidence found and protect it from contamination.

My own immediate concern was with blood, the highly complex substance most commonly found at a crime scene. It is covered by the science known as Serology which studies various body fluids – blood, semen, saliva, perspiration and faecal matter. Some eighty percent of the population are 'secretors', in other words, aside from blood, their body secretions – saliva, semen, urine and sweat carry the same substances as their blood.

The era was pre-DNA profiling but blood could still be grouped, allowing gardaí to narrow their suspect list when trying to track down a criminal.

The Lab needed a branch of trace-evidence specialists to deal with explosives, armed robberies and anything that might have been transferred during the commission of a crime – paint, glass, soil, fibres, hair, shoe prints. In cases involving dangerous driving causing death, the Lab also undertook to examine tachograph charts, which provide information on a vehicle's speed, distance travelled etc. Even fires that have been deliberately set to destroy evidence usually involve the use of an accelerant like petrol, or something which would promote the fire – including incendiary devices. Fires involved a lot of work up to the late 1980s when the Malicious Injuries Code was still in place. This allowed insurance companies to recoup the losses from the State when it was proven that their client had taken sufficient precautions against arson. The code went back to the English common law of levying the local population for the cost of damage in an attempt to discourage the practice.

SCENE PRESERVATION

THE GROUND IS THE GREATEST REPOSITORY of forensic evidence, and the gardaí have been at the forefront of developing preservation techniques. In the past few decades the concept of scene preservation has come into its own, becoming as disciplined as a surgical procedure. Unauthorised voyeurs and members of the press were prevented from tramping over and contaminating the clues left behind. The more vigilant the gardaí became, the more cases we were cracking and the more resources we were able to muster. The number of staff in the Lab increased: from one in 1975, to five in 1978, and more scientists were recruited in 1979.

Our equipment was also improving. We got a scanning electron microscope in 1980 which allowed things to be seen at a magnification of 100,000 times. Ordinary optical magnification can only go up to 400 times. With the new equipment, tiny pieces of evidence could be bombarded with electrons to generate an x-ray whose energy levels were entirely dependent on the sample they were hitting – which also revealed what a substance was composed of. The effect is equivalent to a previously invisible fleck becoming a massive three-dimensional boulder.

There was a great spirit of camaraderie in the Lab in those early days; people were working above and beyond the call of duty, driven by the sense of how much it mattered. When I think of the spirit that drove us on, I also think of May Stynes, the cleaner here who played a considerable part in saving a number of cases after the Lab was flooded in 1984. She also prided herself on making sure the floor was spotless and non slip – such practical considerations are essential but often overlooked. Then there was the Garda Commissioner Patrick

McLaughlin, now in his eighties, who was one of the best pro-
moters of forensic science in the force.

But for all our outlook and staff and equipment, criminals
were also becoming more sophisticated. The idea of going into
somebody's bank account electronically and taking money out
would have been a pipe dream to any criminal who years ago
would have had to go in with a gun and kill someone to get
money. In the same way, who could have foretold in 1980, that
by 1984 it would be possible to get a unique chromosome blue-
print of any person's identity anywhere white blood cells are
found – in blood, in semen in rape cases, in the skin or hair
under a victim's fingernails after a struggle?

The Chinese Gang Murder

THE DIFFERENCE IT MADE TO OUR WORK can be seen in a case
which began in July 1979 when Chinese gang warfare erupted
on the streets of Dublin, leaving one man dead and one battling
for his life. The mêlée involved about fifteen men wielding
knives, machetes, cleavers and clubs. It began in a popular Chinese restaurant on Middle Abbey Street but quickly spilled out
on to the road. Panic-stricken customers of the Curzon cinema
took cover in the foyer. Several gang members fell to the
ground with horrible injuries – blood spurting everywhere. It
was a battle of clans between Cork and Dublin Chinese families. Squads of detectives swooped on the battleground, sending the feuding gang members fleeing down side streets and
laneways. That meant there was blood evidence literally everywhere. The area around the Rotunda Hospital was sealed off
after bloody footprints were found, and gardaí took several
weapons from the scene, including two blood-stained knives,

one a ten-inch butcher's knife. The case demanded all the resources of the Lab – specifically the biology section, which was trying to separate the blood to identify which gang member was where and what part they had played in the fracas. Caucasian blood is different to Chinese blood, which complicated matters, and also the fact that some members of the group were related meant that there were a lot of matches in the old A-B-O blood grouping system. By 1985, all that blood would have been manna from heaven for investigators, but in 1979, it wasn't much use.

But for the Butt!

DURING A BANK ROBBERY on Trinity Street, off Dame Street in Dublin in October 1979, the raider was seen flicking away a cigarette butt as he jumped into a white van. The butt was brought in for examination and from a tiny sample of saliva, Dr Creedon was able to make a blood grouping in the A-B-O system. When a man was apprehended at a later stage in Rathmines, after a member of the public reported someone acting suspiciously in a white van, we found traces of firearms residue on his hands consistent with him having recently fired a weapon. And we could conclusively prove that he was the one who had thrown the butt, and therefore the bank raider, by comparing his blood group with that from the saliva. It was the first instance in this country where saliva was analysed in that way. The case was cracked because of the heady mix of forensic science and luck.

An apple butt proved the undoing of another criminal. The IRA were lying in wait to kill a part-time member of the UDR. A shout came that he was about to drive past and one of the gang, who was biting into an apple at the time, dropped it and killed the victim. The apple was recovered by the RUC. They recognised the distinctive bite in the apple as having been made by a local who had very unusual teeth. A dentist gave evidence of the comparison and the gunman was convicted on that basis.

The Impact of the Drugs Problem

THE SECTION WHICH WAS EMERGING as the fastest growth area for forensics in the mid to late 1970s was drugs, so much so that it was necessary to establish a separate drugs section to analyse substances. Drugs fall into four main types: narcotics, depressants, stimulants and hallucinogens. The word narcotic comes from the Greek *narkotikos*, 'to benumb', and is applied to everything from cocaine to marijuana. Most narcotics, including morphine, codeine and heroin, are derived from opium, which comes from the opium poppy, *Papaver somniferum*. Morphine is a medical painkiller; codeine is an alkaloid made synthetically from morphine and it is commonly used in cough syrups and to alleviate pain with paracetamol. Heroin is made by treating morphine with acetyl chloride. It is usually a white crystalline powder but may be found in cube form and is normally ingested by being heated in a spoon into liquid form and then injected into the blood stream.

DNA

THE BIOLOGY SECTION OF THE LAB is concerned with carrying out DNA profiling.

In the UK, a database of offenders' DNA profiles is stored on computer and will throw up a 'hit' when it finds a match. But in

Ireland DNA profiles can be kept for only six months – the average length of time it takes to complete an investigation and send a Book of Evidence to the Director of Public Prosecutions who decides whether or not to prosecute. The argument is that to keep DNA records infringes a citizen's rights to civil liberties. But I am of the opinion that innocent people have nothing to fear from DNA evidence. In fact, not only does it incriminate the guilty, but it also eliminates innocent people who may be suspected of a crime.

An interesting aside to this debate, and seemingly at odds with the civil liberties argument, is that in Ireland actual fingerprints can be kept for a lifetime.

The Irish authorities are considering giving gardaí the power to take buccal cell swabs from the inside of the mouth, as DNA controls, and allowing the Lab to retain the profiling obtained on a DNA database.

In June of 2000, the Lab started reporting DNA in numbers of a thousand million to one certainty. This is a major development as such results can be regarded as absolute. Techniques have also speeded up and the methods now used give much better statistical results.

PATHOLOGY

THE HUMAN SKELETON FELL INTO the preserve of Forensic Pathology under the exceptional skills of the State Pathologist, Professor John Harbison, based in Trinity College, Dublin. Bones can reveal a person's identity, sex, race, age, injuries and post-mortem mutilation. The length of the thigh-bone can give relatively accurate height. In the late 1970s, forensic anthropologist William Bass began taking the science to its extreme by conducting experiments on the precise rate of human decay. He created the Anthropology Research Facility (ARF), also known as the 'body farm', at the University of Tennessee at Knoxville. Using bodies donated to science, Bass began testing different types of synthesised exposure. Just as in real-life murder cases, he dumped bodies in boots of abandoned cars, in shallow graves and in the open air, and measured the rate of decomposition, recording all the effects of various environmental conditions.

The reason why this research is so important is that murderers often bury bodies to hide them. Here again the dead seek vengeance, since bodies will last longer underground – even when unshielded by a coffin or container – because they are protected from the elements. The general rule for the rate of decomposition is: one week in the open air equals two weeks in water, equals eight weeks underground.

Although Roman Catholics believe that a saint's body will sometimes not decompose after death, in fact this occurs because of environmental conditions such as the protection of a sealed casket within a burial vault. Bacteria thrive in a moist, warm environment. If a body is heavily clothed or deeply buried, the lack of air prevents bacteria from thriving and delays decomposition. Some poisons, such as arsenic, delay putrefaction because they also kill bacteria in the body.

Some bodies are preserved naturally through the circumstances in which they are kept, as in the notable case of the mummy in the hot press.

The Mummy in the Hot-Press

IN 1960 A SIXTY-YEAR-OLD WELSH WOMAN, Sarah Harvey, was

admitted to hospital and in her absence her son Leslie decided to redecorate the house. His mother had been taking lodgers since her husband died in 1938 and the house was badly in need of repair. When Leslie was growing up in the house the hot-press had always been sealed; now he prised it open. Inside he found the remains of a former lodger, Mrs Frances Knight, still dressed in her nightdress and dressing-gown, whom his mother had said moved out in April 1940. The conditions in the hot press were perfect for mummification because of the warm, dry air circulating around the body tissues. When questioned, Sarah Harvey told police that Frances Knight had died naturally and, not knowing what to do, she put the body in the hot press. But the forensic pathologist noted the distinct groove of a knotted stocking around Frances Knight's neck. Detectives also discovered that Sarah Harvey had been claiming her former lodger's maintenance grant every week since her death. She was charged with murder. What she had to say about her conscientious son is not recorded!

Medical Jurisprudence, written by Professor John Glaister, describes what a mummy looks like: 'The whole structure is desiccated, shrivelled, brownish-black in colour, and the anatomical features are well preserved. The skin, which clings closely to the shrunken framework of the body, the hair on the scalp, and the skeletonised features of the face are well preserved. A body in this condition is practically odourless.' In hot climates the drying effect of the hot sand in which bodies were interred also led to natural mummification. Ancient bodies have also been discovered preserved in ice and peat. Infants' bodies concealed at birth also regularly become mummies since the child's body contains few bacteria and has usually been

Forensic experts examining Dr James Donovan's shattered car at
Newlands Cross after Martin Cahill's attempt on his life on 6 January 1982.

Mother and son:
Eileen and James Donovan.

Dr Donovan with Dr Richard Saferstein, who spent twenty-one years as forensic scientist with New Jersey State Police Laboratory, one of the largest crime laboratories in the USA.

The Special Criminal Court at Green Street, Dublin.

Members of the Garda
forensic team in action.

Professor John Harbison,
the State Pathologist.

James Lynagh, the IRA man charged with several brutal murders in the 1980s.
He was shot dead by the SAS in Loughgall in 1987.

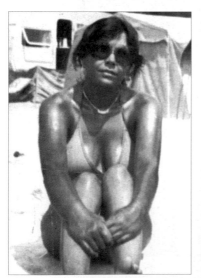

Elizabeth Plunkett, who, like Mary
Duffy, fell victim to serial rapists
John Shaw and Geoffrey Evans.

Marilyn Rynn, who was raped and
murdered after her office Christmas
party on 21 December 1995.

Imelda Riney and Fr Joe Walsh (inset) –
victims of convicted killer Brendan O'Donnell (below).

Footprint of Colm O'Shea, serving forty years for his involvement in the capital murders of Gardas James Morley and Henry Byrne.

Two of the recognised fingerprint ridge patterns –
whorl (left) and radial loop (right).

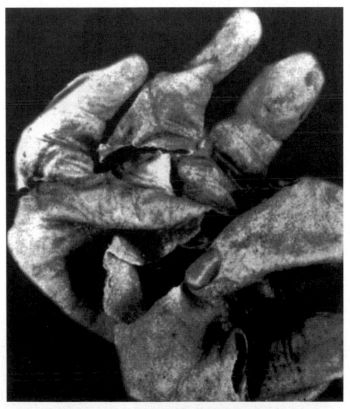

A gruesome clue: a glove of flesh similar to that found
at the Lisdoonvarna arson scene in 1978.

The burnt-out shell of the Stardust Ballroom, where forty-eight young people lost their lives on St Valentine's night, 1981.

The headstone of Martin Cahill, and (below) Cahill in a balaclava and Mickey Mouse T-shirt, which was his usual disguise.

well wrapped up before burial. Some cultures, like those of Ancient Egypt, induce mummification by embalming the body, or treating it with spices for several days after death. This practice was normally reserved for the wealthy, including the pharaohs and their families.

* * *

SOME DISCIPLINES STILL REMAIN with the gardaí and the State Lab, including toxicology, ballistics and fingerprinting. Although I had been involved in the Toxicology Section of the State Lab prior to 1975, the Forensic Lab simply did not have the resources to take over toxicology testing – tests on blood and other bodily substances to establish if they contain foreign substances such as alcohol, drugs or poison. Consequently, the study of poisons remains within the ambit of the State Lab.

When it comes to bullets, the gardaí have the expertise in ballistics – the science of the motion of projectiles. Since gardaí were also the experts in taking fingerprints before the Forensic Lab was set up, this area has also remained with them, although we are housed together now in the Phoenix Park for security reasons.

The rest of the forensic disciplines are covered by experts whose skills are very specialised and so rarely required that it was not necessary to establish actual departments for them in the Lab. These scientists are often attached to universities, places where they can continue their vital research. It falls to the Forensic Entomologist, for example, to identify the species of insect found on a body, as the life cycles of different insects are so regular that they can be used to estimate a time of death.

The Crime That Wasn't

'As a rule,' said Holmes, 'the more bizarre a thing is, the less mysterious it proves to be.'
The Red-Headed League,
Sir Arthur Conan Doyle

I SUPPOSE THAT THOSE OF US WHO ARE so intimately involved with death and human suffering have to develop a certain brand of black humour in the interest of preserving our sanity and also so that we can continue to do our work objectively and scientifically.

And not all the cases which come before us are human tragedies or the result of dastardly deeds. I recall a lecture by Professor John Harbison in which he presented some of the more unusual cases he had come across in his career. At one post mortem on a body found washed up on a beach, a local Sergeant announced: 'Doctor, I think somebody has been here before you.' Sure enough, Harbison found incisions and stitching marks all over the body, which turned out to be that of a woman who had died in England and been subjected to a coroner's inquest to establish the cause of her death. She had been granted her last wish to be buried at sea, but the coffin had burst open and the body surfaced six to eight weeks later!

PART FIVE

FORENSICS, THE CRIMEBUSTER

CHAPTER 12: THE LINDBERGH CASE

'Do you note the peculiar construction of the
sentence – it is the German who is
so uncourteous to his verbs.'
A Scandal in Bohemia,
Sir Arthur Conan Doyle

THE TRUE POWER OF FORENSIC SCIENCE can best be highlighted in the international cases which have been cracked as a direct result of the application of the techniques.

* * *

The case of the century, which demonstrated the power of forensic identification and individualisation, involved the famed aviator, Colonel Charles Lindbergh, otherwise known as 'The Lone Eagle' – the first man to fly the Atlantic solo in 1927 at the age of twenty-five. Lindbergh paid a high price for his fame. His baby son, Charles Junior, aged just twenty months, was kidnapped from the nursery in the family's home near Hopewell in New Jersey on 1 March 1932. The major piece of evidence found at the scene was a home-made wooden ladder, which had been constructed in three sections, each of which slotted into the other, and part of which was broken. A ransom note found on the windowsill of the nursery indicated that the writer had a poor education and, because of the spelling, was almost certainly of German origin:

> *Dear Sir!*
> *Have 50,000$ redy 25,000$ in 20$ bills 15000$in10$ bills and 10000$ in 5$ bills. After 2-4 days we will inform you were to deliver the Mony.*
> *We warn you for making anyding public or for notify the polise.*
> *The child is in gute care.*
> *Indication for all letters are singnature and 3 holes.*

(At the bottom of the sheet of paper there was a drawing of two interlocking circles. Where the circles intersected had been coloured red and three small holes were punched into the design.)

The man who took charge of the investigation was Col. H. Norman Schwarzkopf, head of the New Jersey State Police, and father of 1991 Desert Storm commander, H. Norman Schwarzkopf, Jr.

On 4 March, a second ransom note was received. It scolded Lindbergh for involving the police and upped the amount to $70,000. The Lindberghs paid the $70,000 in gold certificates, through an intermediary, to a man with a German accent who promised the child would be found safe and well aboard a boat called *Nelly* moored on the coast off Martha's Vineyard.

But no trace of the child was found until two months later when his badly decomposed body turned up in a wood two miles from his home. The cause of death was a heavy blow to the head, probably occurring on the night of the kidnapping and perhaps as a result of the baby falling when the ladder broke. This sudden noise – which Col. Lindbergh recalled as sounding as if an orange crate had fallen off a chair in the kitchen – may have been the reason the ladder was abandoned. But it proved the kidnapper's undoing.

Forestry expert Arthur Koehler was asked to help the police. Koehler discovered that the ladder consisted of four different types of wood: North Carolina pine, birch, Douglas fir and ponderosa. Nail holes showed the planks had been used for something else before being fashioned into a ladder. Police sent letters of enquiry to over 1,500 sawmills over the entire eastern US to try and track down the source of the North Carolina pine. It was found to be most similar in make-up to planks from a company in South Carolina which had sold them to forty-six customers in the three years preceding the kidnapping. Detectives visited each one of the delivery sites. At a retail outlet in the Bronx they found storage bins made from North Carolina pine that perfectly matched the wood used in the ladder, but the company kept no customer records and the trail went cold. However, police had notified banks of the serial numbers on the notes used to pay the ransom. One of the notes was handed to a teller in the Bronx by a petrol attendant who had taken it from a customer whose registration he had written on the back of the note because he was acting suspiciously! The car number plate led detectives to a 1930 Sedan owned by a German-born carpenter, Bruno Richard Hauptman, with an address at 1279

East 222nd Street, the Bronx. When police searched his residence they found $14,000 more of the ransom money. Hauptman claimed he was minding the money for a friend who had since returned to Germany and died of TB. Nevertheless, detectives found in his attic a missing floorboard that matched one of the ladder rungs, which fitted perfectly into the space. A study of the grain patterns showed it to be the missing plank. A plane in his garage made tool marks consistent with those found on another part of the ladder.

Hauptman's handwriting was also matched to the ransom note, by comparing his known signature from his auto registration card with a composite signature made up of individual letters from the ransom notes. It was a case of a killer found through compelling forensic evidence. In April 1936 Bruno Hauptman was sent to the electric chair – still proclaiming his innocence.

CHAPTER 13:
WHO KILLED NAPOLEON BONAPARTE?

'It is a capital mistake to theorise before one has data. Insensibly one begins to twist facts to suit theories, instead of theories to suit fact.'
A Scandal in Bohemia,
Sir Arthur Conan Doyle

IN SOME CASES, HOWEVER, the truth is exceptionally complex. The Emperor Napoleon Bonaparte is one of the most famous victims of arsenic poisoning. But how the poison was ingested is not as straightforward as it originally seemed. Two years after his exile to the island of St Helena, Napoleon was showing symptoms of cancer of the stomach – the disease which had killed his father. In March 1821 he was confined to his bed. He died on 5 May 1821 at the age of fifty-two. Post-mortem results seemed to indicate that he died of a stomach ulcer, which may have turned cancerous.

However, as is often the case when such a famous and controversial person dies, speculation and conspiracy theories soon began to spread and rumours of poisoning surfaced. One of Napoleon's servants had cut off locks of his hair some hours after the death and they had been carefully preserved. When traces of arsenic were found in the hair, it led to the charge that the British had deliberately poisoned him. The hair was again tested as recently as 1995 by the Forensic Lab of the FBI and arsenic confirmed.

But another investigator took a different tack. He established that Scheele's Green, a colouring pigment used to dye fabrics and wallpapers from around 1770, contained copper arsenite. An old scrapbook turned up a cut-out section of the wallpaper in Napoleon's bedroom; it was decorated with green and brown rosettes. The green, when tested, proved to contain arsenic. When this wallpaper became damp and mouldy – conditions known to have existed in Napoleon's prison home – it released arsenic in a vapour form into the air. Exposure over a long period could lead to death from arsenic poisoning. The symptoms which Napoleon had been experiencing – vomiting, stomach pain and loss of body hair – are also symptoms of arsenic poisoning. Napoleon's room was apparently a death chamber.

CHAPTER 14:
THE MYSTERY OF THE ROMANOVS

> 'The evil that men do lives after them, the
> good is oft interred with their bones.'
> Julius Caesar, *William Shakespeare*

IF PRESIDENT MIKHAIL GORBACHEV had not declared a spirit of openness, *glasnost*, in the 1980s, the truth about what happened to the Russian royal family might never have been revealed. Russia's last Tsar, Nicholas II, was forced to abdicate in March 1917. In the civil war that ensued shortly afterwards, the socialist leader Vladimir Illyich Lenin resolved to assassinate the Tsar, his wife the Tsarina Alexandra Feodorovna, their four daughters the Grand Duchesses Olga, Tatiana, Maria, and Anastasia, and their thirteen-year-old son Alexis Nicoleivich, the Tsarevich, who was a haemophiliac.

On 16 July 1918 the family, together with servants and the family physician, were executed in a cellar in Siberia in a hail of bullets. Those who did not die immediately were bayoneted. The corpses were loaded on to a truck and thrown into an abandoned mine shaft some twelve miles from the town of Ekaterinburg. When word got out, the authorities ordered the relocation of the bodies, afraid that if the story was authenticated there would be a swell of sympathy for the old regime. The corpses were hauled out of the mine with ropes, taken to another site in the town, hidden under a pile of logs and doused with hydrochloric acid. It was intended to burn the bodies in order to destroy any prospect of identification, but the process was botched because of the high cost of fuel and fears that those involved would be seen. Only two of the bodies were burned; the others were buried.

Many Russians preferred to believe that the family was still alive rather than accept that they had been murdered in such a barbaric fashion. And this fantasy was aided by a woman who threw herself into the Landwehr canal in Berlin in 1920. When rescued she was committed to the Daldorf Asylum where she refused to give her name. However, after eighteen months, the woman made an astonishing claim: she was the Tsar's youngest daughter, Anastasia. She did bear a strong resemblance to the grand duchess, and a former lady-in-waiting to the Tsarina provided a positive identification. The woman could not speak Russian, but she claimed she was suffering from amnesia. As early as 1927, a private investigator concluded that she was a Polish peasant, Franziska Schanzkowska, a factory worker with a history of mental illness, who had vanished three days before the mystery woman was pulled from the canal. 'Anastasia' renamed herself Anna Anderson but maintained her claim until her death in Charlottesville, Virginia, USA, in 1984 by which time she had acquired celebrity status.

Thanks to Gorbachev, secret documents – including an account of the assassination by Yacob Yurovsky, the commander who had given the orders to shoot – became available.

These were researched by filmmaker Gely Ryabov who worked for the Interior Ministry. In 1979 he located the Romanov remains under the same pile of logs in which they had been buried, and, while he was convinced that they were authentic, he felt that the matter was still too contentious, and waited a full decade before going public in 1989.

In 1992 the Russians asked American forensic experts for assistance in identifying the remains of the skeletons. The team assigned to the work included a forensic anthropologist and a hair and fibre microscopist.

In all, they examined nine skeletons, five female and four male. The skulls were badly fractured, probably by bullets, making facial reconstruction impossible, as it involves building the various layers of flesh on top of the bone structure.

Nevertheless, the team was able to make tentative identifications. The pelvis of the first body showed it to be a fully-grown female. According to William R. Maples, one of the forensic experts involved, the ankle joints showed an extension of the joint surfaces as if the woman had spent many hours crouching or kneeling, 'perhaps while she was scrubbing'. The body was identified as most likely that of the Tsarina's maid, Anna Demidova.

The second body was that of a mature man. The skull lacked upper teeth, consistent with having had an upper dental plate, which Dr Eugene Bodtkin, the doctor who accompanied the little Tsarevich, was known to have.

The third body was that of a female in her early twenties. The shape of the head with its bulging forehead agreed with the photographs of the eldest daughter, the Grand Duchess Olga.

The fourth skeleton was of a relatively short, middle-aged

man. 'The hipbones showed characteristic wear and deformation produced by many hours on horseback and we know the Tsar was an ardent horseman.'

The tips of the root molars (wisdom teeth) on the fifth body, a female, were incomplete and the limbs had only just finished growing, consistent with its being the nineteen-year-old Grand Duchess Maria.

The sixth body also belonged to a female. An examination of the extent of pelvic growth put her age at a minimum of eighteen years, while her collarbone suggested an age of at least twenty. Her height, at five feet, five and a half inches, was in between that of the other two females. On the balance of probabilty, the remains were identified as the Grand Duchess Tatiana, twenty-one years old at the time of her death.

The seventh body was identified as the Tsarina because of her 'amazing and exquisite dental work'. She had two crowns made of platinum, others of porcelain and 'wonderfully wrought gold fillings'.

The eighth body was 'grievously damaged by acid', but was identified, mainly by a process of elimination, as the Tsar's footman. The ninth body was also thought to be another of the family's servants.

But since the body of Anastasia had not been found, it was still necessary to prove beyond any doubt that Anna Anderson was not telling the truth, which was where state-of-the-art technology came in. In 1993 DNA tests were done using mitochondrial DNA taken from the bones of Tsarina Alexandra and a sample donated by Queen Elizabeth of England's husband, Prince Philip, and ex-King Considine of Greece, as both are maternal line descendants of Queen Victoria and thus related to Alexandra, who was a grand-daughter of Victoria's. When their DNA was compared, the result was matched with a probability of almost 99 percent. Anna Anderson's body had been cremated, precluding DNA testing. However, she had had an operation in 1979 at the Martha Jefferson Hospital in Charlottseville and the hospital retained a pathology specimen of tissue. DNA from this tissue was first compared with a Romanov sample and did not match. But when the tissue was compared with DNA from Karl Maucher, a maternal grandnephew of the Polish factory worker Franziska Schanzkowska – identified by the private eye many years previously – the result was a positive match.

Eventually, in July 1998, eighty years after the assassinations, the Romanovs could be given a proper burial. Their bodies were laid to rest in St Catherine's Chapel of SS Peter and Paul Cathedral in St Petersburg.

CHAPTER 15: MARTIN BORMANN
The Missing Nazi

AT THE NUREMBERG TRIALS IN 1945 Martin Bormann was sentenced to death by hanging for his substantial participation in Nazi war crimes. But Bormann was not sitting in the dock with his infamous co-accused, including Hermann Goering, Rudolf Hess and Hans Frank. In fact, no one knew where he was. Martin Bormann had, effectively, disappeared off the face of the earth.

In his absence, the investigation proceeded on the basis of voluminous documentary evidence linking him to the expulsion of millions of Jews to Poland, and the use of Ukrainian women as slave labour.

A ruthless, power-hungry and brutal man, Bormann, whose official job was as Hitler's secretary, exercised more influence on Nazi policy than anyone else. He replaced Rudolf Hess as Hitler's Deputy in Charge of Party Affairs after Hess was asked to resign from the Party following his secret flight to England to negotiate peace.

Bormann was forty-five years old when he vanished at the end of the war. His fate became one of those unsolved riddles, surfacing every now and then in newspapers and books. Sightings of him were reported from South America, where he was alleged to be in the company of the notorious Auschwitz doctor, Josef Mengele. There were other reports from Russia and from parts of the Arab world.

But the truth was much simpler. At the beginning of May 1945, a skeleton rumoured to be Bormann's, had been found in Berlin. The man had been shot. But it wasn't until the development of DNA that the identity of the skeleton could be revealed. Bone tissue from the remains was compared with that of a Bormann aunt and a scientist declared that he was 99.9 percent certain that the bones were those of Martin Bormann. Fifty-four years after the war's end, the riddle was solved.

The allegedly much-travelled Bormann had never left Berlin at all. He had been with Hitler and Goebbels in the bunker on 30 April 1945. When they committed suicide, Martin Bormann fled in an effort to escape the advancing Soviet Army. He didn't get very far.

Martin Bormann's son, Martin Jr, a godson of Adolf Hitler, had converted to Catholicism and become an ordained priest in 1958, spending many years as a missionary. Nowadays he travels all over Germany, giving lectures with titles such as 'Fascism: Never Again'. When his father's remains were returned to him in 1999, Martin Jr, afraid that a grave would become a place of neo-Nazi pilgrimage, had his father's bones cremated. In August 1999 what was left of Martin Bormann was scattered at sea in international waters.

PART SIX
FORENSICS ON TRIAL

*'For lawyers, jurors and judges a forensic
scientist conjures up the image of a man in a
white coat working in a lab, approaching his
task with cold neutrality, and dedicated only
to the pursuit of scientific truth.
It is a sombre thought that the reality
is sometimes different.'*
(Regina v. Ward, 1993)

CHAPTER 16: THE BIRMINGHAM SIX

THE BIRMINGHAM SIX CASE WAS PROBABLY the single most destructive blow to forensic science in terms of public perception on this side of the Atlantic. The notorious forensic scientist, Dr Frank Skuse, used the antiquated and discredited Greiss test to prove that two of the accused had been in contact with nitroglycerine – explosives. Under pressure, he claimed he had 'modified' Greiss, but his modifications were never subjected to any scientific scrutiny. In other words, he was using his own highly dubious test to justify his own results.

Emotions were running at fever pitch following the explosions in Birmingham in November 1974, when twenty-one people were murdered and 162 wounded in the worst IRA atrocity in Britain since the beginning of the Troubles. Two and a half hours after the blasts, six men were arrested at Heysham: Paddy Hill, Billy Power, Hugh Callaghan, Gerry Hunter, Richard McIlkenny and John Walker. The public outcry threatened to turn into a full-blown anti-Irish pogrom. The accused men's families found nooses around their gates with hate messages saying: 'Hang IRA bastards'. Their friends' homes were vandalised and the Six themselves were beaten up mercilessly by the prison staff and inmates.

But it was the prejudice shown by the court which caused the most irreparable damage to the concept of British justice. At the trial, Justice Bridges said the forensic evidence was 'absolutely critical' in the prosecution case. Yet the swab from an unreliable test had shown positive results only from the right hands of Billy Power and Paddy Hill. This, said Dr Frank Skuse, made him 99 percent certain that both Power and Hill had recently been in contact with explosives. These positive 'explosive' traces from the right hands were then subjected by Skuse to a much more powerful test known as GCMS, one hundred times more sensitive than the Greiss test, but both registered negative. Yet Skuse stuck to the Greiss result and maintained in court his certainty that the men had been handling bombs.

At the Old Bailey on 15 August 1975 the Birmingham Six were convicted on multiple counts of murder and were sentenced to life imprisonment: 'You stand convicted on each of twenty-one counts, on the clearest and most overwhelming evidence I have ever heard, of the crime of murder.' The words of Justice Bridges were unequivocal.

In 1985 the Granada television programme *World in Action* commissioned two forensic scientists to carry out the Greiss test on a variety of substances – hair lacquer, cigarette packets and old playing cards – all of which the men were known to have been in contact with before their arrest. All gave positive results. Yet the appeal judges clung to Skuse's evidence and the Birmingham Six were not released until March 1991 after serving nearly seventeen years in prison. In 1992 the Court of Appeal decided that Dr Skuse's conclusion was wrong, and demonstrably wrong, judged even by the state of forensic science in 1974.

CHAPTER 17: THE MAGUIRE SEVEN

THE CASE OF THE MAGUIRE SEVEN is another blatant example of where pressure for a conviction under extreme provocation can play havoc with the criminal justice system. Annie Maguire was an aunt of Gerry Conlon, one of the Guildford Four, and her house was put under observation because of this association. When nine people gathered in the house for a funeral, police waited until late in the evening to raid. Each of the nine had their hands swabbed to test for explosives residue. The forensic scientists claimed to have found nitroglycerine on the hands of seven of them. Since the house had been under tight observation for between twelve to sixteen hours, the bomb-making substance would have had to have been handled by the seven before that. I could never detect nitroglycerine after a few hours had elapsed, let alone twelve. All traces can be washed away with just soap and water. The other aspect is that the technique used by the forensic scientists in this case was thin air chromatography, which is quite a good technique, but would require a reasonable amount of the substance. There is no way a substance passed around seven people would have been present in such an amount, especially twelve hours later. Finally, the easiest part of making a bomb is pushing the soft, gooey, putty-like gelignite around the mechanism. It requires only one pair of hands. So what were seven of them supposed to have been doing? It is beyond statistical probability that, with nine people in a house, seven of them would attach and deal with the nitroglycerine, which only needed to be handled by one.

When these inherent contradictions were eventually exposed, the British responded by saying that all seven must have used a roller towel, which had been contaminated by whichever of the party handled the supposed bomb. But no nitroglycerine showed up on any tests of the roller towel. Swabs taken from Annie Maguire's hands were clear but she was convicted on the basis that her household gloves – that she wore when washing up because she suffered from dermatitis – had traces of nitroglycerine. The gloves had been kept in a drawer, frequently used by everyone in the house, seven of whom were supposed to have given positive results, so it was a spurious argument.

Both the Maguire Seven and the Birmingham Six were treated badly by forensic science but in the latter case it was because of an individual: Dr Skuse, with his bizarre spot tests and highly selective decision to ignore the results of genuine, recognised tests. When Annie Maguire's conviction came up for review, it was reviewed on a completely different issue. The British justice system was simply not prepared to admit that it could be wrong. Forensic science alone was made to take the blame.

CHAPTER 18:
THE TRIAL OF OJ SIMPSON

ALL THE EVIDENCE AND ALL THE POWERS of deduction in the world are not enough if a jury does not, or chooses not to understand it.

In court, forensic evidence is communicated to non-specialists through an expert witness. My good friend and the leading forensic scientist in the United States, Dr Richard Saferstein, said that the OJ Simpson case showed that even more important than a good scientist in a court case must be a good communicator. All kinds of witnesses can say all kinds of facts, but the jury has to understand and believe them. The witness has to be credible. If Hitler said something to you, even if it were true, what credibility would he have?

The case began on 12 June 1994 when a dog started barking at the home of Nicole Browne Simpson, the divorced wife of black celebrity OJ Simpson, a former professional football player, movie star and Hertz Rental ad man.

Her body was found alongside that of twenty-five-year-old Ronald Goldman, a restaurant waiter who happened to be in the wrong place at the wrong time. He had called to her home on the night of the murder to return a pair of glasses which Nicole's mother had left in the restaurant earlier in the day. Both had suffered multiple stab wounds.

Police travelled to OJ Simpson's Rockingham Avenue estate only a few miles away to inform him of the murder. The lights were on, but Simpson was not home. He had flown to Chicago on business – apparently in quite a hurry. Police discovered blood on the door of his white Ford Bronco and a trail of blood leading from his front door. A dark brown leather glove was found between the outside wall and a fence. This right-hand glove matched a left-hand one found at the scene of the crime at Bundy Drive. Nicole had bought them at Bloomingdales in Manhattan in 1990.

Informed about the slayings, Simpson agreed to return. He was wearing a bandage on the middle finger of his left hand. This injury was an issue because a trail of blood dripped along to the left of the bloody shoeprints that were found heading away from the murder scene. In the shoeprints was found blood belonging to Nicole Browne and Ron Goldman, but the blood in the trail belonged to someone else. It seemed that the killer must have sustained an injury to his left hand. This blood was analysed and contained Simpson's DNA. It had been collected before Simpson's own blood was obtained and therefore could not have been planted as his lawyers later suggested. Simpson gave different stories about how he had cut himself – a good indicator of a poor liar. And his blood was also found in his car, along with Nicole's and Ron Goldman's. Blood was collected from his driveway, foyer and master bedroom. A pair of his socks also had bloodstains. An FBI expert identified the killer's shoe from the bloody footprints as being a size twelve and coming from an exclusive and very expensive Italian designer. Photographs were produced which showed OJ wearing shoes belonging to the designer and matching the description. A blue cap found at the scene contained blond hairs like Nicole's and black, negroid hairs like Simpson's.

Apart from these links, OJ Simpson had a record of abusing his wife; there were forty-three incidents over seventeen years. A transcript of a 911 call from Nicole on New Year's Day in 1989 showed Nicole to be in fear for her life. When her safety deposit box was opened after her death it contained documentary evidence of her abuse at the hands of her husband – colour photographs of her bruised face, diaries filled with accounts of his beatings and stalkings, and letters from him apologising for what he had done. She had also made a new will a month before her murder.

Simpson had no alibi. A limo driver saw him arriving at the house after the murders but OJ claimed he had been inside all the time. When the warrant was issued for his arrest he led police on a sixty-mile slow-speed chase, captured live on television. While his friend drove, Simpson lay in the back of the vehicle, holding a pistol to his head. He had thousands of dollars, a fake beard and a passport to make good his escape. He had left a note saying: 'Don't feel sorry for me. I've had a great life, great friends. Please think of the real OJ and not this lost person.'

But despite such compelling evidence, what matters at the end of the day is what goes on in court and Simpson had assembled a 'dream team' of defence attorneys. He pleaded not guilty to the charge of first-degree murder and so began what became known as the DNA wars. Three different labs matched the blood from the trail of drops beside the footprints to Simpson's – a one in 170 million chance that it might have been anybody else's. The defence argued that the blood samples obtained had degraded, been switched or contaminated – hinting at outright conspiracy to frame an innocent man.

The prosecution struggle was to make the complexity of DNA sound easy. Then the defence played the race card. Taking advantage of one cop's denial of ever having used the word *nigger*, they showed him to have lied. And the defence chose not to put Simpson on the stand to face tough questioning from the prosecution. Yet the jury took only four hours to reach a verdict: Not guilty. The Goldmans and the Brownes consolidated their separate civil actions into a single case. Civil actions require proof by a preponderance of the evidence, rather than proof beyond a reasonable doubt as in criminal cases. The jury did not have to be unanimous, nevertheless they were. OJ Simpson was found responsible for the deaths.

Richard Saferstein believes the issue arising out of the OJ Simpson case is whether the forensic evidence presented in the courtroom was consistent with the involvement of OJ Simpson.

'Now I know, based on my own experience, of no other crime scene where there was so much physical forensic science evidence left that pointed to the involvement of one man, the one man in this case being OJ Simpson. I want to say one thing about science. It is objective. It is colour blind. We have no axe to grind in the laboratory. We call it as we see it,' he said.

All the technology in the world is not enough if the science is not forensic – made suitable for court.

PART SEVEN
CAPITAL CRIMES AND CAPITAL PUNISHMENT

'... Death sentences are cruel and unusual in the same way that being struck by lightning is cruel and unusual.'
Justice Potter Stewart
(US Supreme Court, Gregg vs Georgia)

THERE WAS A TIME WHEN EXECUTIONS WERE a public spectacle. The condemned man or woman would meet their death in front of a cheering crowd, and the authorities had no qualms about their actions. In England, the 'Bloody Code' was a list of over 200 capital offences that were punishable by death, including being in the company of gypsies for one month and 'strong evidence of malice' in children aged between seven and fourteen. We are a long way from that time now. In the twenty-first century, the death penalty is possibly the most controversial practice within the judicial system. It is an emotive issue and one which carries with it much debate and conflict.

Many countries have opted to discontinue the practice – by 1999 sixty-five countries, including the EU member states, had abolished the death penalty. Of those countries that continue to execute criminals, the United States of America is very much to the forefront. The first recorded execution in America was of Daniel Frank, put to death in 1622 having been convicted of theft. Frank was to be followed by many fellow citizens: between 1930 and 1999, 4,459 people were executed in America. (Official records for capital punishment in America begin in 1930.) It continues to be a hugely contested practice, with Amnesty International waging an ongoing campaign to abolish capital punishment worldwide. Executions command massive media attention, such as the execution of Oklahoma bomber Timothy McVeigh, while the debate continues to rage about the merits of putting criminals to death.

Prior to the twentieth century in Ireland, the sentence of hanging, drawing and quartering was handed down fairly regularly, as was the sentence of public hanging. However, the twentieth century saw a shift in attitude as politicians responded to the ethical dilemma posed by State executions. Accordingly, Ireland abolished the death penalty in 2001 by referendum.

CHAPTER 19: AN EYE FOR AN EYE
The Death Penalty in Ireland

SINCE 1900, 126 CAPITAL SENTENCES have been handed down in Ireland. A total of forty-seven people were hanged for the murder of fifty-three victims. Twenty-nine persons sentenced to death by the civil courts were hanged, and of the six sentenced by the special courts one was hanged and five were shot. Between 1946 and 1964, eighteen people, including three women, were sentenced to death, but of these only three men were hanged. The last execution in Ireland took place in 1954.

Many of Ireland's executions were carried out by Albert Pierrepoint (1905–1992), Britain's most prolific executioner, also known as 'Number One'. He earned his nickname because when he was around, other hangmen only ever 'assisted', that is, they would strap the accused's arms and ankles and place a hood over his or her head. But it always fell to Number One to pull the lever that released the trapdoor on the scaffold.

Albert Pierrepoint came from an established dynasty of executioners – both his grandfather and granduncle were hangmen. His grandfather, Harry, had been a butcher by trade and a hangman in his spare time. Whereas Harry's style was to make his clients feel at home and pass a cheery comment before seeing them off, his successor – his elder brother Tom – displayed no such niceties. Tom was more offhand, a style the authorities preferred. In the course of his career he carried out 102 executions, as against Harry's toll of seventy-eight.

But these figures pale in comparison to Albert's, whose emphasis on time and weight turned the job into a performance of skill and mathematical accuracy. Albert Pierrepoint hanged over 680 men and women. He gained international notoriety following the Nuremberg trials in 1945, when Nazi war criminals were convicted of crimes against humanity. Mr Pierrepoint was one of the hangmen contracted to execute some of the many people found guilty.

Pierrepoint lived in the seaside village of Southport, Lancashire, where he owned a pub called 'Help the Poor Struggler', but he was on call to travel to Mountjoy Jail, Dublin, to carry out executions. He often boasted that he could perform an execution, take a three o'clock flight from Dublin and be opening his pub by half-past five. Success, for Pierrepoint, was always measured in terms of speed: he timed himself from the moment he put his hand on a condemned man or woman's shoulder in a cell to the moment when his or her neck snapped on the gallows. Pierrepoint's record for a hanging was seven-and-a-half seconds. He had perfected his craft through meticulous attention to detail. Every condemned man or woman's drop distance was calculated in direct proportion to his or her weight – the key to making death instantaneous.

In the late 1940s Pierrepoint taught the executioner's craft to an Irish hangman-in-waiting at Strangeways Prison in

Manchester. But the man, whom Pierrepoint knew only by the alias of Thomas Johnston, was 'not up to the task', he later claimed. In his autobiography, *Executioner Pierrepoint* (1979), Pierrepoint stated that Mr Johnston did not have the stomach for his job, and Number One was always called in when he got cold feet.

> *'I did not think he [Thomas Johnston] had the character to be an executioner. He was old and short and timid. When I took him into the execution chamber at Strangeways Prison, his face went white as chalk. But I gave the basic training and he went back to Ireland. Two months later, the governor of Mountjoy wrote to say that he had a man under sentence of death and he would be obliged if I would act as an assistant to Mr Johnston.'*

Mr Johnston had been asked by the governor of Mountjoy to carry out the hanging and had replied to the request in writing:

> *'I am prepared to officiate should it take place, but without acting alone, I think that I explained to you about a year ago, that I should like to assist at say one more, as you are already aware the only practical experience I've got is of attending one, and that was about one year and nine months ago (at Strangeways), as you know this is not something one sees every day and while I am sure I could carry it out at the same time, I am not perfectly sure of myself, and it would never do for anything to go wrong. The first time I was speaking to you before leaving Dublin you assured me that our friend would come over for one or two more.'*

However, when it came to the crucial moment, poor Mr Johnston lost his nerve and buckled, leaving the unflappable Pierrepoint to take over and finish the job. As Mr Johnston's appointment was never rescinded, he became the only executioner in Europe who never performed an execution!

Executioner Pierrepoint also contains the hangman's views on capital punishment, which, for a man of his trade and dedication, are remarkable: 'I do not now believe that any one of the hundreds of executions I carried out has in any way acted as a deterrent against future murder. Capital punishment, in my view, achieved nothing except revenge.' However, he conceded that hanging was 'the most humane and dignified method of meting out death to the delinquent.'

Albert Pierrepoint holds the distinction of being the man who performed the last execution in Ireland, and the last execution of a woman in Britain, that of Ruth Ellis. Ellis was executed on 13 July 1955 at London's Holloway Prison. She was charged with the murder of David Blakely, a racing car driver. Her fate was sealed when the counsel for the prosecution asked: 'Mrs Ellis, when you fired that revolver at close range into the body of David Blakely, what did you intend to do?' and she nonchalantly replied: 'It is obvious that when I shot him I intended to kill him.'

The last man hanged in the Republic was twenty-five-year-old Michael Manning from Limerick. Manning had been convicted of the murder of Catherine Cooper, a sixty-five-year-old nurse. Manning's confession shows the terrifyingly random nature of many crimes:

> *'I saw a lady walking in front of me towards Limerick, on the left-hand side of the road. I walked behind her for a few minutes. I suddenly lost control of myself and jumped on her because I saw she was alone. She let a few screams, I knocked her down on the grass. I pulled her into the grass margin and stuffed grass in her mouth to stop her from roaring. She got quiet after five minutes,*

but she began to struggle again, and asked me to stop. She just
said 'Stop, stop.' The next thing a motor car with lights stopped
beside me. I got up and jumped over the ditch.'

Manning was executed by Pierrepoint on 20 April 1954 in Mountjoy Jail. On that occasion Number One turned to the assembled prison officers and two priests and declared: 'I love hanging Irishmen – they always go quietly and without trouble. They're Christian men and they believe they're going to a better place.'

I have no explanation for how the phrase 'he wouldn't drop for Pierrepoint' ever came to refer to a man slow to put his hand into his pocket to buy a round of drink, but it probably has something to do with being very thick-skinned and hard-necked.

As an interesting aside: a relation of Albert Pierrepoint is a Church of Ireland curate based in Dublin. His ancestor may have culled those of the flock who strayed, but the curate seeks to prevent the wayward from ever leaving the pen!

Albert Pierrepoint retired in 1956 and there were no more executions in Ireland. Death sentences were handed down after this time, but popular opinion was changing and such sentences were always commuted. In 1964 the last death sentence for a murder of a non-garda was given to Shan Mohangi, a South African student studying at the Royal College of Surgeons in Dublin. Mohangi was convicted of a gruesome murder: he stood accused of killing and dismembering his eighteen-year-old Dublin girlfriend, Hazel Mullen. However, his sentence was commuted and he was deported to South Africa, where he is now a respected politician.

After the Mohangi case, the Irish government abolished the death penalty, except for the murder of gardaí, prison warders, foreign heads of state, members of foreign governments and diplomats.

The death penalty was abolished from Irish statute law under the Criminal Justice Act 1990, and finally removed from the Irish Constitution after a referendum in June 2001. On this occasion the Irish people voted to remove all reference to the death penalty from the statute books, thereby agreeing that it can never again be invoked, regardless of circumstance.

CHAPTER 20:
THE MURDER OF
GARDA MICHAEL REYNOLDS

*'I have done the State some service
and they know't.'*
Othello, *William Shakespeare*

DISCUSSION ON THE PROS AND CONS or rights and wrongs of capital punishment is necessary and beneficial, but nothing can prepare you for an active role in the decision on whether a particular person lives or dies. Certainly, some acts are so destructive that they invalidate some citizens' right to take their place under the sun. But these things are never easy to come to terms with. Twenty-six years ago I had to deal with my first capital crime, and therefore had to confront my own beliefs on the question of the death penalty. The case concerned the murder of Garda Michael Reynolds.

Michael Reynolds was from Ballinasloe, County Galway, and had been five years in the force. On 11 September 1975, Garda Reynolds left his home in Artane with his wife and four-year-old daughter to collect his wages from Raheny Garda Station. The thirty-year-old garda was rostered for night duty and was not due in work until later that evening. Consequently, he was not in uniform.

Just before 4pm the family was approaching the Bank of Ireland in Killester Shopping Centre when a green Ford Cortina swerved dangerously in front of them. Garda Reynolds presumed it had just been stolen and set off in hot pursuit. The car had indeed been robbed, but it had been taken from outside the Irish Hospital Sweepstakes in Ballsbridge, and not from the bank in Killester, as Garda Reynolds probably assumed. What he could not have known was that the car had been stolen for a specific purpose: armed robbery of the Bank of Ireland in Killester. If he had known that he was actually following armed bank robbers with £7,000 hot money stashed in the car, he would no doubt have thought twice about giving chase in the company of his wife and young daughter. But had he thought twice he would have been in dereliction of his duty. Instead, Garda Reynolds came across a crime and reacted as he was trained to do: to protect those around him.

In contrast, the bank raiders were intent on wrecking the community. Styling themselves 'anarchists', they were members of an organisation called Black X, which had been set up in opposition to society and all its institutions: its sole aim was to undermine society. Although it was a gang of four who carried out the raid, two of the people in the car that day – a modern-day Bonnie and Clyde, Noel Murray and his wife, Marie – were the brains behind the raid.

Noel Murray was born on 12 December 1949 in County Kildare and was the youngest of seven children. He went to national school in Leixlip, County Kildare, and to Maynooth Secondary School. He left school after his inter cert, attended Bolton Street College of Technology and went on to become an apprentice with CIÉ as a metal fabricator. In 1966, aged just seventeen, he joined the Republican movement.

His wife, Marie Murray, née Finlay, was born on 21 October 1948 and was adopted at an early age. She also grew up in Kildare, but was an excellent student and got five honours in the Leaving Certificate followed by a job in the Civil Service. Between 1966 and 1973 she worked in the Department of the Gaeltacht, but under the employment rules of the Civil Service at the time, she had to leave when she married Noel Murray. In 1968 she joined Sinn Féin as a housing and Irish language activist.

As a couple, they had made a nuisance of themselves before they ever graduated to serious crime. They had lodged High Court applications, apparently with the intention of clogging up the overworked system rather than achieving anything. One such application was lodged to force the State to take them off the waiting list for council housing and provide them with accommodation before they were too old to have children. This was the same State that they declared they did not recognise, but at the same time believed owed them a living.

The Murrays resigned from Sinn Féin in 1973 and devoted themselves to campaigning on behalf of the militant Prisoners' Revenge Group, which targeted prison officers. They raised funds for Black X through armed robberies and built up a deadly stockpile of explosives and ammunition.

On the day of the Killester robbery they were joined by two other men. Marie donned a long blond wig and a home-made balaclava fashioned from the type of green military material used in combat jackets. Noel disguised himself with a false beard, drooping moustache, sideburns, a wig and a pair of sunglasses. Each carried a brown pillowcase in one hand and a Colt .45 in the other. The second man, also disguised, accompanied them into the bank. The third man stayed in the getaway car and kept the engine running.

Inside the bank, the cashiers were petrified. One, Patricia Haran, thought that she would collapse and had to be helped to a chair by a colleague, Margaret Wilson. Noel Murray told her: 'Don't worry, I won't harm you,' but he brandished his gun threateningly as his wife moved behind the bank counter and began to stuff money into the pillowcases.

Unknown to the raiders, Patricia Haran had inadvertently marked the money – she had doodled the totals on the top of each bundle as she counted and sorted them. Her scribble was to prove as effective as all of today's top security methods in providing invaluable forensic evidence.

When Marie Murray had filled the pillowcases with £7,000, the trio raced outside and jumped into the waiting getaway car. The Bank of Ireland staff phoned the gardaí immediately, and some ran out to see if they could catch the Cortina's registration number.

It was at this point that Garda Michael Reynolds happened upon the scene and sped after the fleeing raiders. Within minutes, the Cortina screeched into St Anne's Park in Raheny, taking a corner on two wheels at 45mph, before hand-braking to a sudden halt. The occupants scattered out of all four doors, spreading in different directions and leaving behind remnants of the robbery that would help seal their fate.

Garda Reynolds also jammed on his brakes, checked to see that his wife and child were unhurt and then took off on foot after the front-seat passenger: Noel Murray. Reynolds's wife watched as her husband ran from her view, past the clock tower and into the trees. Children playing in the area and a corporation park ranger looked on in amazement.

Garda Reynolds was fit and managed to catch up with Noel Murray near a bridge over a stream. He grabbed him and forced him to drop his weapon, which was retrieved by Marie Murray, who now held two guns. She pointed one at Garda Reynolds's head from a range of thirty inches and screamed, 'Let my fella go!' Then she fired a single shot. One of the children who had witnessed the chase compared the noise to the sound of a plank of wood hitting the ground, but from her car Mrs Reynolds recognised it as the sound of gunshot. It was a sound that announced the murder of the nineteenth garda killed since the foundation of the State in 1922.

Garda Michael Reynolds fell to the ground. The Murrays wrenched off their disguises and fled in different directions. Noel jumped onto the first bus that came along – a 29A to Donaghmede – before re-routing and making his way home to Raheny. His wife had reached home before him.

Police back-up and an ambulance were on the scene almost immediately. Paramedic Gerard Bell saw Garda Reynolds lying on his back with his feet almost in the stream. His eyes were closed and blood was gushing over his face from an open wound in his forehead, soaking his T-shirt and seeping into the ground around him. His pulse was very feeble. Beside his body lay a single button, along with a left-hand black glove, a black nylon coat, a pair of sunglasses, a false moustache, a green balaclava and a wig. Fourteen yards away lay a pair of gold-rimmed glasses. All of this evidence was delivered to me at the Laboratory.

At 6.10pm Garda Michael Reynolds was pronounced dead at Jervis Street Hospital. Dr Niall Gallagher, the consultant pathologist who performed the post-mortem, declared what everybody knew: death resulted from lacerations to the brain caused by a gunshot wound. But there was one question the post mortem couldn't answer: who had pulled the trigger?

The Murrays had discarded an incredible amount of forensic evidence at the scene, ensuring we had a strong lead to follow. Gardaí brought to the Lab everything recovered from the abandoned Cortina, including a black-handled hairbrush, a piece of nylon stocking, a dark blue handbag, a false beard, a false moustache, a pair of sunglasses, a bunch of keys, a blue button, a contact lens case, a vial of glue and a compact. I also personally attended the crime scene to check for clues or evidence, and from the car mat I removed a sample of grit, which would be essential should the suspects be located early and their shoes recovered.

We had an awful lot of evidence, but the police had no suspects. However, the contact lens case taken from the car was found to hold two lenses. When the lenses were examined, we were able to ascertain the myopic prescription of one of the criminals. A dragnet of opticians in the area threw up an exact match – Marie Murray of Grangemore Estate, Raheny.

In the meantime, Christine Doyle, a cleaner hired to maintain the public toilets on Marine Road in Dun Laoghaire, made an unusual discovery. In one of the cubicles she found a bag marked *Terenure Cleaners*, which contained two brown nylon pillowcases, a false moustache, two green balaclavas, a grey woollen hat, a light brown jacket and a bundle of coloured money bags. She handed the bag and its contents over to the gardaí, who brought them to me.

By comparing fibres, I was immediately able to link the items found in the toilet to those found in the abandoned car. Now all that was needed was to find out if they could be linked to the suspects. I told the gardaí what I would require: items such as clothing, wigs, hairs, contact lenses or saline solution to compare with similar items found at the crime scene.

About a month after the murder the gardaí began staking out the house in Raheny where Marie and Noel Murray lived. The behaviour of the occupants was suspicious: they only ever emerged early in the morning or late at night, and always accompanied by a large Alsatian dog, which never left their side. Against a records check, gardaí discovered that Noel Murray, who was using the alias Noel Finlay, was a wanted man (he had failed to comply with a bench warrant issued for his arrest), and that his wife had also come to their attention in the past for handling stolen money (£500) and being in possession of firearms.

At 7.30am one morning, when the couple left on one of their walks, gardaí moved in with a warrant to search the premises.

They delivered to me a number of items they hoped would link the Murrays to the getaway car or to the area where Garda Reynolds had been murdered. Things that would normally seem like harmless household items were now vital evidence, posing a threat to the Murrays's very lives – a contact lens case, a bottle of contact soak, a lady's coat, a red hair brush, a reel of thread, a pair of stockings, a false beard and moustache, side-burns, two hairnets, a bottle of mastic gum, a lady's nylon night-dress, a green combat jacket and a lady's right-hand black glove. Explosives were found in the hot-press, as well as an ashtray containing eight bullets.

The couple returned at 8am and Noel Murray immediately unleashed the guard dog on the detectives; the dog had to be shot dead. Noel Murray then reached into his jacket, but gardaí overpowered him. They searched his jacket and found he had been reaching for a pistol. The pair were then formally arrested in connection with the murder of Garda Michael Reynolds. Noel Murray simply replied: 'I knew this day would come sooner or later.'

I immediately began tests on the items recovered from the crime scene and from the house. The hairbrush found in the getaway car contained a number of man-made fibres, which matched in colour, composition and thickness the false moustache and beard found in the Murrays's house; the wigs had obviously been brushed quite vigorously before the raid. Vanity was to prove Marie Murray's undoing. On the compact found in the car I discovered the same gum as had been used for the false moustaches and beards. A bottle of this same gum, Mastic Spirit Gum (normally found only in dressing-rooms of theatres) was found in the Murrays's bedroom. Marie must have touched up her make-up just before the robbery, using her compact, inadvertently transferring gum from their disguises onto it. There were also traces of the gum on the thumb of the lady's black glove found in the park beside Garda Reynolds's body.

The lady's glove taken from the house was the same design and had the same lining as that found beside Garda Reynolds's body. The fastening studs on both had the same stamp. They were the same size. Both left- and right-hand gloves had the same degree of wear, indicating that they were the same age. I had no doubt that they were a pair.

I found that the moustache from the public toilet in Dun Laoghaire was similar to the beard found in the park, and that glue stains on the right-hand pocket of the combat jacket found at Dun Laoghaire matched the adhesive already identified.

The home-made green balaclava was stitched with a pale mauve thread, and gardaí recovered a reel of the same colour thread from the house. I found that the same thread had also been used to sew a tear in the brown jacket found in the toilet in Dun Laoghaire, where the other two accomplices must have fled and ditched their disguises.

The litany of matching evidence went on and on. Contact lens saline solution taken from the house matched exactly in composition the fluid in the lens case found in the car. The button recovered from beside Garda Reynolds's body was of precisely the same make as those on a blue gabardine coat retrieved from the house, which also happened to be missing its top button.

A pair of tights recovered from the house was the same colour, composition and density as a cut-off section found in the car. I found the portion in the car had been stretched more than one would expect with normal wear. It was probably used as a makeshift balaclava – a common disguise in armed robberies.

In the grit taken from the vehicle I found pine needles, which were also present in the pocket of the green combat jacket taken from the house. The gold-rimmed glasses found at the scene matched Marie Murray's prescription.

The explosive substance taken from the hot-press at the Murrays's house turned out to be a mixture of nitroglycerine and ammonium nitrate – a dangerous explosive known as Frangex, or, in layman's terms, dynamite.

Two cartridge cases found in the house had the same physical and chemical characteristics as a spent case found at the scene in St Anne's Park, and I concluded that they were from the same batch of manufacture.

The bullet removed from Garda Michael Reynolds's head matched a bullet found inside the hot-press, in that they had exactly the same appearance and silver-and-copper composition, suggesting that they came from the same batch and manufacturer. There was a slight difference in weight, but this could be accounted for by the fact that the bullet that hit Garda Reynolds would have displaced some metal when it hit bone.

In all there were nine definitive forensic links between the Murrays's house and the scene of the murder. There was no doubt in my mind that there was a connection between Noel and Marie Murray and the murder of Garda Michael Reynolds.

Husband and wife were kept in custody while the investigation continued. Gardaí purposely kept them apart and the strategy worked. Marie Murray was interviewed in Ballymun Garda Station by Detective Inspector John Finlay, Noel Murray was interviewed in Harcourt Terrace Garda Station. Marie was anxious to cooperate. She cried briefly and then composed herself, announcing: 'I will tell you a lot about it but not everything'. She alleged that the two other men involved in the raid were Ronan Stenson – a friend of her husband's – and a friend of Ronan Stenson's whom she refused to identify. Eventually, she alleged that the elusive fourth man involved in the robbery was a restaurant owner in Dublin, well-known to the police as a Republican sympathiser. However, no charges were ever brought against this man.

Marie was asked who had fired the fatal shot. She put her head in her hand and cried for a moment. After about thirty seconds she looked straight at the detective and pointed at her own face. But, she insisted, the killing was accidental.

'I did it. It was panic and carelessness. I did not know he was a garda until I heard it on the news. I only intended to hit him. He crumpled up. I moved in to take Noel from him. I think I made a swipe at him. As I made the swipe the gun went off. There was a shot and the man crumpled up. I could not believe what happened.' She claimed the weapon used was at home under the mattress. Gardaí went back to the house and recovered the gun.

Next she was shown the wig found beside Garda Reynolds, and she had no hesitation in admitting that she had seen it before, indicating that she had last seen it 'on Noel, on September 11.'

Following her interview, Marie was asked to sign her statement, but she refused, saying: 'Noel would be mad at me. He told me never to sign a statement.' However, she was courteous and anxious to assist and wrote the final lines of the statement in her own handwriting, concluding with the words: 'I do not intend to sign the statement now, but maybe later.' It was as good as a signature.

Gardaí now allowed her to see her husband. Following their meeting, during which she learned that Ronan Stenson was claiming he had been beaten in custody, Marie Murray backtracked. She now claimed that she had been subjected to 'mental torture' while in custody and that the statement she had given was untrue: 'I laid it on a bit thick to protect Noel. They wanted me to name a fourth person and suggested that I was protecting this person because I was carrying on with him. To put it in a nutshell, they called me a whore.'

Noel was also alleging that he had been physically tortured. He refused to eat or drink while in custody, claiming that his food had been poisoned. He maintained that he had been punched by four gardaí who held his head in the bowl of a cell toilet and threatened to drown him.

In the Special Criminal Court the judges didn't believe the Murrays's new version of events and proceeded to admit into evidence the statements they had made in custody. Noel's statement alleged that when he had entered the Bank of Ireland in Killester: 'I was carrying a gun. It was fully loaded. I stood inside the main door and ordered the staff to move back from the counters. I was pointing the gun towards the ceiling in the bank. The two people with me, one male, one female, took what money they could find. They were both carrying cloth bags. They put the money in the bags. The three of us left the bank.'

His statement continued with a description of the shooting: 'I heard a voice shout "stop" and then I heard a bang like a shot and the man who was holding me fell to the ground at the side of the stream.' His wife, he said, was on the ground at the time. 'She must have slipped. I knew at the time that she was carrying the stolen money from the bank and two guns, my one and her own. We headed off in different directions.'

Immediately the gardaí set about working on the weapon recovered from the house, which Marie Murray had admitted was the one she used to kill Garda Reynolds. She had claimed it went off accidentally. Contrary to her claim, gardaí found that the trigger pressure was seven pounds, which meant that the weapon was safer than most and deliberate pressure would have been required in order to discharge it. Analysis of the path the bullet had taken when it entered Garda Reynolds's head was not consistent with the gun having been fired while she was 'swiping' at him. The trajectory was straight, indicating that the gun had been held level with his head and fired. There was no distortion of the angle of entry, which would have been expected if the gun had gone off unintentionally.

Noel and Marie Murray, together with Ronan Stenson, were put on trial for armed robbery and murder in the Special Criminal Court, and all three pleaded Not Guilty. The Special Criminal Court operates on a unique basis in that there is no jury. Instead there is a panel of judges who hear the case and pronounce a decision.

However, Stenson's case took a different turn after he suffered a complete nervous breakdown in court. He had resisted arrest and gardaí admitted that in the ensuing scuffle he had 'suffered a few bangs' before being interviewed in Clontarf Garda Station. Stenson alleged that police officers had threatened to take him into the mountains and 'give him what he gave Reynolds'. On the ninth day of the trial, Stenson collapsed while in the witness box being questioned by his own barrister, Paddy McEntee SC. An army doctor examined him on behalf of the court and was satisfied that his injuries were 'consistent with having been punched or kicked' in the ribs.

During further court appearances, Stenson appeared to be sleepy in the dock and the court was advised that he had been dosed with 4mg of Valium, two Aspirin and one Mogadon just to get him there. A psychiatrist testified that he was unfit to stand trial, claiming he was unable to exist in the present, was repeating suicide wishes and was trembling violently.

The judges decided to put Stenson's trial off and go ahead with the Murrays's trial. When Noel and Marie learned that Stenson was to have a separate trial, they became aggressive and extremely disruptive. They dismissed their lawyers, described the three judges as 'fascist vultures' and declared the court to be a 'fascist tribunal'. Marie Murray described the trial as a 'lynching party'.

When requested to take the oath, Noel Murray repeatedly replaced the word 'court' with 'tribunal'. He said the oath was nothing more than 'a device to give credence to perjury'. Noel further declared: 'This is not a court of law. It is a sentencing tribunal of a fascist State. I would not insult my solicitor or counsel by asking them to proceed with this farce ... The attitude has been "hang the Murrays" because the Murrays and the police know they are anarchists. We are completely opposed to the State and all the State's institutions. We will fight against these institutions with every means at our disposal and we will not submit to this farce anymore ... For the past three weeks this has been a most entertaining circus, but the tragedy is that it is our lives, or the best years of them, not to mention our marriage.'

Marie displayed just how much hold her husband had over her by reneging completely on earlier efforts to help police: 'We are anarchists,' she avowed, 'we have no interest in the State except to abolish it ... I have a right to be judged by my peers, the people of this country, not by three prosecutors appointed by a fascist State to sit on a bench.'

The Murrays disrupted proceedings continually. They used their hands to drum on the dock and shouted abuse until eventually they had to be removed to the cells beneath the court. Microphones and loudspeakers were rigged up there, to allow them to listen and partake in the proceedings. They were given every opportunity to rejoin the court if they were willing to 'behave'. But they continued to scream and act in a manner inappropriate for the courtroom.

Before passing judgement, the presiding judge, Justice Pringle, posed a question fundamental to sentencing: if the Murrays had not known that Garda Reynolds was a garda when they shot him, could they still receive the death penalty? The defending barristers drew attention to a case in Ontario, Canada, which decreed that an attacker must know that his or her victim is a policeman and is on duty in order to receive the death penalty. However, in every other Commonwealth country the opposite view prevailed. The common law, that is, law based on precedence, was particularly strong in Ireland where the gardaí, in consequence of being unarmed, required added protection.

In his summing up for the State, Noel McDonald SC said that the question of manslaughter should be ruled out, because in their statements the Murrays had admitted that the gun was loaded and fully cocked. Capital murder , he added, meant the murder of a garda acting in the course of his/her duty – a criterion fulfilled in this instance.

It is reasonable to conclude that at the point in time when Garda Reynolds gave chase to the Cortina, he could not have been motivated out of selfishness. Nor was he giving chase to protect his wife and child, as, prior to the chase, they were not in any immediate danger from the occupants of the car and, indeed, the whole situation must have been terrifying and distressing for them. Any right-minded person has to concede that when Garda Reynolds made the decision to follow the car he did so out of a sense of social conscience – to try and prevent anyone getting hurt. In other words, he did it for the rest of us. Since he died defending the State, in theory his murder is deserving of the State's ultimate punishment. But, as he was dressed in civilian clothing, it was not an open-and-shut case: the raiders claimed they did not know that they were shooting at a garda; however, Reynolds's colleagues believed he would have shouted at them, 'Stop, police', or some similar warning to identify himself.

The trial lasted three-and-a-half weeks. The judges deliberated for seven hours. Returning for sentencing, Justice Pringle declared that Noel and Marie were guilty and should pay the ultimate price for their crime: death. The date set for the execution was 9 July. Noel Murray was to be executed at the Curragh Military Detention Camp; Marie was to be executed at Mountjoy Jail, Dublin.

Marie Murray, her eyes glistening and her voice shaking, announced that she would like to thank the court for vindicating every word she and her husband had said 'since starting this farce'. Noel Murray remarked that no evidence had been produced at the trial to show that Garda Reynolds was attempting to arrest the people he had followed or to let the people know why he was arresting them. It was the closest he had come to a public confession.

The Murrays were the first married couple ever sentenced to death in the history of the State. It was a pivotal moment in terms of Ireland's changing self-perception. Despite the Church's pronouncements against the death penalty, and the fact that capital punishment contradicted the Roman Catholic idea of unconditional brotherly love, public sympathy for the Murrays was nil. They had a remarkable way of remaining unpopular even when facing the hangman's noose. For the first time in a long time the Church did not hold sway.

As it turned out, Ireland found itself unable to vent its rage against the Murrays. The judiciary intervened on the occasion of their appeal by commuting their death sentences to life imprisonment. They were both released in 1992 after serving seventeen years of their life sentences. Ronan Stenson was later acquitted.

CHAPTER 21:
THE MURDERS OF
GARDAS MORLEY AND BYRNE

IN 1980 THE THORNY ISSUE OF CAPITAL PUNISHMENT was again on the agenda when two gardaí were murdered in Roscommon in the course of the country's most infamous bank robbery. This time there was no grey area: one garda was in uniform and both had emerged from a squad car, so there could be no mistaking their identity when the trigger was pulled. It was precisely because they were members of the force that Detective Garda James Morley and Garda Henry Byrne were gunned down in cold blood.

On 7 July 1980, three men planned a daring bank robbery over drinks in the luxurious Cloonabinna Guest House Hotel, overlooking Ross Lake in Moycullen, ten miles from Galway City. It may not have been in their plans that day, but their actions would result in a callous double murder that met the criterion for the death penalty.

On that day at the Cloonabinna Guest House Hotel, staff recalled that the three men who stayed in the hotel immediately prior to the robbery had used large denomination notes – £50 and £100 – and that money was no object. They also recalled how a fourth man had joined them one evening, but this man had never been identified.

One of the plotters was twenty-eight-year-old Colm O'Shea from Cork City. O'Shea was born into a family that would never have expected him to take the path he chose. His father was a noted professor of science in University College, Cork, and when O'Shea also began to study science in his father's alma mater, it was expected that he would follow in his illustrious footsteps. But although he was reared against the backdrop of academia in his comfortable middle-class home, on campus O'Shea was drawn to the left-wing politics of the Irish Communist Party, and he established links with the Irish Republican Socialist Party. After less than a year of study, he dropped out of college.

O'Shea first came to the attention of the police following a robbery at the Pye Ireland factory in Dundrum, south Dublin, for which he got six years in the Curragh prison, County Kildare. He was granted eighteen months' remission, and it was during that time that he became involved in the bank robbery.

The second man in the party at the hotel was thirty-four-year-old Patrick McCann from Dungarvan, County Waterford. He was born Michael Burke, one of a family of ten, but changed his name by deed poll to Patrick McCann after several run-ins with the law for possession of offensive weapons, theft, burglary and breaking and entering. In 1979 he crashed a roadblock in a stolen car with false number plates and was convicted and disqualified from driving for twelve months, but restored on appeal. McCann had been wanted in connection with a number of crimes prior to the bank raid. He was also known to be closely associated with the provisional IRA, although he was based in Scotland.

The third plotter was alleged to have been forty-two-year-old Peter Pringle, but his convictions have since been quashed and the State decided against pursuing a new trial. Pringle was a fisherman and a familiar figure in Galway, due to his imposing physical appearance: he was 6ft 4ins tall and had a distinctive white beard.

Pringle was born in Ringsend in Dublin in 1938. His father was a garda, as was his uncle. He emigrated to England after minor skirmishes with the law and ended up as a pub manager in Luton, Bedfordshire. He returned to Ireland in the mid-1960s and became manager of a confectionery shop in Thurles, County Tipperary. He was allegedly involved with the Irish Republican Socialist Party and the Irish National Liberation Army. He was arrested in 1977 and again in 1978 under Section 30 of the Offences against the State Act, but was released each time. He moved from Donegal, where he had fished on trawlers based in Killybegs, to Galway. There he skippered a converted car ferry, *The Severn Princess*, which operated a regular ferry service between the Aran Islands and Rossaveel on the Connemara mainland. At this point he separated from his wife, leaving her and five children in Davern, England, and moved in with a woman in Moycullen.

In the hotel, O'Shea, McCann and a third man banded together to work out the finer details of their plot. They had received a tip-off that £56,000 had been delivered to the Bank of Ireland branch in Ballaghadereen, County Roscommon, in the middle of the night during the previous week.

Gardaí would later form the view that the INLA had brought these men together, but that their subsequent actions had not been sanctioned by the organisation. The gang executed the robbery plan with military-style efficiency. Two Ford Cortinas were stolen, one white and one blue – one from the car park of the Ardilaun Hotel in Galway and the second from Athenry. They drove the cars to a County Council dump less than two miles outside Roscommon town, passing the shrine village of Knock on the way, and left one Cortina, the white one, at the dump site.

They travelled to the bank in the blue Cortina. Two of the robbers, carrying handguns and wearing balaclavas, entered the bank, while a third stood guard in the street outside, armed with a single-barrel shotgun. Inside the bank, McCann and O'Shea bundled £46,500 into black plastic sacks. Outside, the third man showed not one hint of panic when a uniformed garda happened upon the scene. He simply ordered him to lie down on the ground, which the garda did.

When McCann and O'Shea exited the bank, the three jumped into the Cortina and sped away. A lorry driver ahead of them stopped to chat with another driver and blocked the road, and again the raiders reacted with cool efficiency, simply reversing and setting off in another direction. Their first destination was the dump, where they abandoned the blue car and set it on fire to destroy any forensic evidence. They continued to make good their escape in the second, white vehicle.

Only a chance-in-a-million encounter upset the plan.

The alarm call to Castlerea Garda Station had been received at 2.40pm. The message relayed to all squad cars was that the Bank of Ireland in Ballaghadereen was being held up and that a garda was lying prostrate on the ground outside, under the muzzle of a shotgun.

Four gardaí were despatched: Garda Derek O'Kelly drove the four-door black Escort, with a garda sign and flashing blue beacon on the roof; in the passenger seat was Sergeant Michael O'Malley; sitting immediately behind him was Detective Garda John Morley; with Garda Henry Byrne beside him, sitting to the rear of the driver's seat.

Shortly after leaving the station, the gardaí stopped to get petrol. They were heading for Loughlynn when a message came through on the radio that the raider's Cortina, a blue Mark II model with the registration number VZI 168, was travelling in the direction of the dump and there was no longer any point in heading for Ballaghadereen. The gardaí began to travel cross-country to try to cut them off, turning right at Aghaderry Cross. As they approached the Shannon Cross intersection, Garda O'Kelly reduced speed to take the right-hand turn. Hedges and undergrowth blinded his view, and suddenly a white Cortina came slamming into his right front.

The collision was not severe and the bank raiders travelling in the Cortina – two in front, both wearing balaclavas, and one in the back – acted swiftly and with ruthless decisiveness. The driver seemed to stoop down as if to hide his face, then reversed two yards. A man got out of the front passenger side. In his gloved hand he carried a shotgun, which he aimed directly at the gardaí in the Escort. There followed a blast from the shotgun and a succession of bullets riddled the patrol car.

From their position in the front seats, Garda O'Kelly and Sergeant O'Malley had a full view and immediately ducked, covering their heads with their hands and yelling to their colleagues in the back to do the same. Instantly the windscreen shattered. Next came indiscriminate firing at the patrol car with what sounded like revolver shots. When the burst of fire ceased, Garda O'Kelly lifted his head and saw the white Cortina reversing up the road. Only the two hooded raiders were still in the car, the rear passenger was on foot and running towards bushes.

Detective Garda Morley had been hit in the chest but was not seriously wounded, and he jumped from the car. He shouted 'hold it' and fired a warning shot. Garda O'Kelly followed him, but shattered windscreen glass had lodged in his shoe and he could not keep up with his colleague. Back in the car, Sergeant O'Malley opened his door and found Garda Henry Byrne lying on the ground outside. He was turned partly onto his left side, with his legs bent up to his stomach and his head facing the front of the car. Sergeant O'Malley called to him but Garda Byrne did not answer. Blood was oozing steadily from a gaping wound in the back of his head where a bullet had exited.

Much had happened in the space of just a few seconds. The reversing white Cortina came to a halt about seventy yards from the garda car. Two tall men with masks got out and ran into the adjoining field towards the main Loughglynn/ Ballaghadereen Road.

Sergeant O'Malley radioed the station to alert them to what had happened. He asked for immediate back up, and requested a priest and ambulance to be despatched to the scene. He then knelt beside his dying colleague and whispered an Act of Contrition into his ear.

But the carnage was not over yet. Sergeant O'Malley heard more gunfire, and he realised that Detective Garda John Morley was firing his gun somewhere up ahead. Garda O'Kelly was struggling to pull off his shoe to dislodge the glass when he caught a fleeting glimpse of his colleague, Morley, through a gap in the bushes. He shouted to him to 'be careful'. Morley was twenty-five to thirty yards ahead of him now. He saw him stop, level his gun and shout 'hold it' to the two men he was chasing in the field. Garda O'Kelly could see nothing else because a hedge obscured his view. But he heard a blast from a shotgun and three to four bursts from Detective Garda Morley's gun. He saw his colleague tumble back onto the roadway and disappear; he took cover under a hedge. Detective Garda Morley fired one last time, this time hitting Colm O'Shea in the chest.

Approaching this dreadful scene, ambling down the road from the Loughlynn direction, came a red Volkswagen Beetle, towing a trailer with five lambs. Garda O'Kelly knew its owner to be seventy-two-year-old retired garda Michael Kneafsey. Kneafsey's twenty-seven-year-old son, Thomas, was driving. Garda O'Kelly waved his arms at the men and ran towards them, but as the vehicle slowed down the two raiders suddenly sprang from the ditch on either side, wielding their guns and beckoning the Kneafseys to stop, shouting, 'Out, out'. One of them put his gun through the partly opened window on the passenger side and pointed it at the elderly widower. The ex-garda asked him, 'What is this about?' and the gunman answered, 'Get out or we will soon let you know.' Thomas Kneafsey tried to calm things down by assuring the robbers that they were getting out, which father and son then did.

One of the gunmen attempted to shove the elderly farmer into the back seat of the car, telling him that he was about to be taken hostage. Thomas Kneafsey asked the gunman what he wanted with an old man, telling him to take him instead. In the confusion, Michael Kneafsey seized his opportunity. The ex-garda grabbed one of the gunmen, but as he did so, a shot went off in the direction of the ground. Thomas Kneafsey cried out as if he had been hit, and fell down. Thinking his son had been shot, Michael Kneafsey stopped struggling and the gunmen quickly removed the trailer from the Volkswagen and sped off.

Meanwhile, Garda O'Kelly raced to the place where he thought Detective Garda Morley had dived for cover. Instead, he found him badly injured and only semi-conscious. Garda O'Kelly shouted back to Sergeant O'Malley, 'John has been hit', and that two of the raiders had hijacked a red Volkswagen. O'Malley relayed the information on to the station. Thomas Kneafsey gave the registration number of his car, which Sergeant O'Malley also radioed to base.

Garda O'Kelly comforted his colleague, telling him that he would be all right. The Kneafseys joined the two gardaí. Michael Kneafsey held the wounded guard's hand and heard him tell O'Kelly, 'I feel very bad'. Detective Garda Morley had lost a critical amount of blood. He had been hit by a shotgun blast that had severed the main artery in his left leg. Another car was flagged down and the motorist went to get help. John Morley's last words were: 'Say goodbye to my kids and wife for me.' Michael Kneafsey whispered the Act of Contrition into his ear as the thirty-eight-year-old father of three died on the road-side. A priest arrived and performed the Last Rites.

The scene at Shannon Cross was one of utter devastation. The police car was riddled with bullet holes. The white Cortina was embedded in a telegraph pole, its front and back windscreens shattered. But by far the most chilling sight was of two young gardaí – Henry Byrne and John Morley – lying dead, callously gunned down in the course of their duties. Their deaths brought to a total of twenty-one the number of gardaí who had been murdered since the foundation of the State.

Gardaí were soon on the trail of the murderers. The red Volkswagen was found abandoned in Ballinlough, where yet another car had been stolen, which in turn was later abandoned in Coonfad. The raiders were spotted turning away from a checkpoint at Loughlynn, about ten miles away. A full-scale manhunt immediately got under way.

Colm O'Shea, who had been hit by a bullet from Morley's gun, was found a short time later outside a farmhouse, not far from the crime scene. He was bleeding from a wound in his chest. He was taken to Galway Hospital for treatment, and was released six days later and taken in for questioning. Patrick McCann managed to escape the dragnet for forty-eight hours, but was arrested at a checkpoint at Frenchpark, County Roscommon, just seven miles from the murder scene. Twelve days later, gardaí went to the housing estate where Peter Pringle lived, entered his house through the kitchen window and arrested Pringle in an upstairs bedroom.

While the manhunt was in progress, the Lab had begun its work of collecting and analysing forensic evidence from the crime scene. The first task was to examine the bodies of gardas Morley and Byrne. I cannot put into words the effect that being present at Detective Garda John Morley's post mortem had on me. It was extremely distressing to see a public servant, as were we all in the Lab, reduced to such a state simply for carrying out his duties. Detective Garda Morley's demise was violent and unecessary, and I think every person present that day was wishing they did not have to perform this task. It was vital, however, that all bullets be recovered so that a forensic case could be built against the perpetrators, so we had to put aside our feelings and comb every inch of his body for remnants of shotgun pellets. The post-mortem of Garda Byrne was also difficult to face, but it was more straightforward in that the garda had been shot through the head and died instantly. These cruel and premature deaths drove me and my colleagues to work harder to identify the perpetrators of this heinous crime.

Some of the evidence removed from the scene was quite unusual. An entire mound of clay was removed from a ditch near the crime scene because it contained the impression of the seat of the trousers of one of the raiders, which had been moulded into the ground as he crouched down in the earth behind a wall. For the three months until the trial I sprayed that half-tonne of soil with a fine mist of water four times a day, seven days a week, so that the imprint of the raider's Farah slacks in the mud would hold. Keeping the imprint damp stopped it from sinking under its own weight, and bought me time to make a comparison between it and the clothing worn by each of the three. At the time, there were three different and distinct weaves in this type of trouser, reducing the likelihood of it having been made by anyone else. Through endless visual comparison I found conclusively that the impression in the mud matched McCann's trousers. The patterns on the soles of his footwear also matched shoe imprints found in the mud.

Detectives also found footprints on the counter of the bank in Ballaghadereen, left by one of the three raiders as he vaulted over it. In all there were five impressions on the counter, some complete, some partial. I concluded that they had been made by a runner worn by Colm O'Shea. All of the prints sported a diamond-shaped pattern, which matched Colm O'Shea's rubber-soled shoes. The first footprint was of a left shoe, and it was the same size (size ten) as O'Shea's, and the overall pattern, plus worn areas and defects, corresponded perfectly. A partial heel print also had points of similarity with his footwear.

In one of O'Shea's pockets I found four small fragments of dark red domestic gloss paint, which appeared to match similar fragments from the rear seat of the white Cortina that had been abandoned at Shannon Cross. Spectrographs of the samples – which give readings as reliable as fingerprints of the composition of the substance tested – showed the fragments to be identical to the flakes of red paint found in McCann's pocket, thus locating him in the getaway car. In fact, the clothing of all three accused men was found to contain the same flakes of paint. The source of the paint was unclear, but nonetheless it meant all three had been together just prior to their arrest.

Pieces of broken windscreen glass found in O'Shea's pocket had refractive indexes matching the glass of the getaway car, narrowing the likelihood of the glass having come from any other windscreen.

Dr Tim Creedon conducted a microscopic examination of fibres found in the white Cortina and concluded that they were the same as fibres from McCann's clothes.

Six wine-coloured wool fibres found in the Cortina and the Volkswagen were microscopically examined and found to match the wool of Pringle's jumper. Dr Creedon extracted dye from the wool fibres and from the wool jumper, and found that they were also the same. (This evidence was later contested in court.)

A hair lifted from the floor of the Cortina matched the head hair of Colm O'Shea. It was the same length as O'Shea's hair and had been recently cut. The sample was very dark in colour, very heavily pigmented and had the same diameter as O'Shea's hair. The chances of the head hair sample belonging to anyone else were about one in 4,000.

Liam Fleury analysed firearms' residue swab tests taken from O'Shea and McCann, and these indicated that the two had been in contact with recently discharged firearms. Fleury found similar residue traces on their clothing. When subjected to the firearms' residue tests, a balaclava, which had been shown to contain head hair from O'Shea and fibres from McCann's trousers, also proved positive. We also found the men's fingerprints on ordnance survey maps left in the car.

Two shotgun cartridges were found on the roadway, about five feet from the patrol car, one live and the other spent. More spent bullet shells were found on the rear seat of the patrol car, and these were positively linked to the weapons the raiders had been carrying.

But, as I have said before, how you are judged and understood in court is as important as what you have found, and after all the Lab's efforts, the greatest test was now to come. At the trial all three defendants pleaded Not Guilty to the charge of capital murder of Garda Henry Byrne, Not Guilty of the capital murder of Detective Garda John Morley and Not Guilty of the armed robbery of £46,500. Once again the issue was one of life and death. This time the courts would not save the men if found guilty and it fell to the government to rescue them from the hangman. But was the government prepared to take a stance on such an emotive double murder?

McCann's barrister, Paddy McEntee SC, claimed that the forensic findings were 'disreputable gobbledegook' and 'unscientific'. While cross-examining Dr Tim Creedon about his findings, McEntee asserted that it was scientific *opinion*, not scientific *fact*, that the head hair would match a sample from only one person in every 4,000 of the population. 'Are we to take this without one pick of scientific data?' he asked. Dr Creedon replied that he had based his conclusions on his opinion as an expert. Dr Sheila Willis, also of the Lab, stated that she had no doubt that a footprint shown in evidence was made by the left runner of Colm O'Shea. McEntee countered that it should be borne in mind that the footprint came from a mass-produced shoe.

In relation to fingerprint evidence, the defendant's barrister claimed that the forensic evidence was inconclusive. He argued that there was no way of knowing how long the fingerprints had been on the maps, and that the presence of the men's fingerprints on the maps did not mean the men had murdered the two gardaí and robbed the bank.

In relation to the spectrographs of the wool fibres, the forensic evidence was dismissed as 'circumstantial'. Peter Pringle's legal team argued that the wine-coloured wool fibres could have come from any similar pullover. They added that the paint on his clothes did not connect him to the abandoned car. The defence team was satisfied that the evidence was not conclusive beyond a reasonable dout.

As the case was heard in the Special Criminal Court, it was not a jury trial. The evidence was presented to legal experts and the presiding judge, Justice Liam Hamilton. After deliberation, the judges returned to deliver their verdict. Referring to the case against Colm O'Shea, Justice Hamilton said he was satisfied that when the defendant was found, injured, and asked by gardaí if he had been involved in the bank robbery, he replied, 'Yes, I was.' The judges accepted that it was O'Shea's footprint on the bank counter. They agreed with Liam Fleury's finding that the bullet taken from O'Shea's chest wound was of the same calibre as the bullets fired from Detective Garda Morley's gun at the scene, just before he died. And the judges also accepted that swabs taken from O'Shea's hands showed traces of firearms' discharge residue, conclusively linking him to the scene.

The judge referred to the answer O'Shea had given when asked by gardaí if he wanted anything: he said he 'wanted arsenic, that is how I feel about it.' Asked to what he was referring, he said 'the shooting'.

In Patrick McCann's case, the judges found that fingerprints and a palm print on a map of the area found in the getaway car were both made by the defendant. Fingerprints from another map in O'Shea's possession were also made by him. They believed that traces of firearms' residue found on his trousers and jacket linked him to the scene, and they admitted into evidence a number of statements by McCann declaring he 'was sorry' and he 'would be satisfied to get away with ten years' and that he 'hadn't slept much since the crime'.

The judge said that the remaining forensic evidence against McCann was not of such a degree of certainty as to base a conviction on, but that it was consistent with his involvement.

In the case of Peter Pringle, the presiding judge declared that the court believed he had made a statement to the gardaí – which he later contested – saying: 'I know that you know I was involved, but on the advice of my solicitor I'm saying nothing and you will have to prove it all the way'. The court was satisfied that Pringle was aware of what he was being accused of when he made this statement. Justice Hamilton believed that wool fibres taken from a jumper that Pringle had admitted wearing on the day of the shooting matched fibres found in the two Cortinas and the Volkswagen, and thereby linked him to the crime scene. The judge also referred to the fact that fragments of red paint found on Pringle's coat matched red paint fragments found in the getaway car, and further that traces of firearms' residue were found on his trousers.

The trial lasted six weeks. In pronouncing sentence, and in contrast to the Murray conviction, the presiding judge declared that it was 'beyond reasonable doubt' that the persons who fired the shots did so in full knowledge that the patrol car was occupied by gardaí acting in the course of their duty, and that the defendants' actions showed they intended to kill or cause serious injury to these gardaí. For the last time in Irish criminal history a judge would pronounce: 'You are to be removed from this court to the place where you were last confined, there to be detained in custody to December 19 and there suffer death by execution in the manner prescribed by law.'

Two of the men smirked; the third gave a clenched fist salute. All three were transported to death row in Portlaoise Jail. They were, however, granted leave to appeal the decision, and it was this that saved their lives, since if there is no hope of reprieve it is considered more humane to hang condemned prisoners within a week to ten days of their sentence, so they do not suffer unduly. The appeal led to the sentences being revoked by the government. All three condemned men had their sentences commuted to forty years' imprisonment without remission.

Pringle continued to proclaim his innocence and waged a long campaign against his sentence. In May 1995 the Court of Criminal Appeal quashed his convictions and ordered a new trial. A week later, the State announced that it would not proceed with a new trial, and he was released. He has since been granted the right to sue the State for wrongful conviction and incarceration.

The funerals of Garda Henry Byrne and Detective Garda John Morley were attended by four bishops, 112 priests, the taoiseach Charles Haughey and seven cabinet ministers.

Morley, from Knock in Mayo, had played Gaelic football for his county. A statement from the GAA in Mayo read: 'John Morley is immortal in the memory of Mayo for his long service of dedication to our country, but even more so for his own bearing and deportment during the years of that service. Because of his massive frame and strength he was seldom given due credit for the honesty and fairness of his play. He was big in every sense of the word.'

Henry Byrne was also from Knock. He was aged twenty-nine and was married with two children. His wife was expecting their third child at the time of his murder. He had spent most of his garda service in Carlow. After the shootings a colleague said: 'They just wanted to see the law of the country respected.'

PART EIGHT

CASE STUDIES – THE ROLE OF FORENSICS IN IRELAND'S MOST NOTORIOUS CRIMES

CHAPTER 22:
THE SERIAL RAPISTS
Shaw and Evans

IRISH SOCIETY HAS CHANGED IRREVOCABLY over the past three decades. The 'Troubles' have made a large contribution to the climate of fear, but there are other threats to the national community. Crimes against women have become more frequent and more vicious in recent times. Sex crimes are reported almost daily in the newspapers, each more shocking than the last. This was not always the case – there exists in my memory an 'old Ireland' when community and individuals were respected. In my mind, the case that cleft the old Ireland from the new began on 28 August 1976, when a twenty-three-year-old Dublin woman, Elizabeth Plunkett, stormed out of the packed McDaniel's pub in Brittas Bay, County Wicklow, after a row with friends.

Two Englishmen, John Shaw and Geoffrey Evans, had just left Jack White's pub (later to become notorious as the location for the arranged murder of the proprietor, Tom Nevin, by his wife Catherine, in March 1996), which was just a few miles from

McDaniel's, when they saw Elizabeth walking alone in the darkness. She didn't stand a chance. The pair were seasoned criminals and were wanted at the time by the British police in connection with the rapes of three women. In Britain they were branded as serial rapists; in Ireland they would be branded as the perpetrators of two of the most horrific sex crimes ever reported.

John Shaw was a thirty-one-year-old labourer from Wigan in Lancashire, who had worked in the Lancashire coalmines as a teenager. He had twenty-six previous convictions, mainly for larceny, but also for indecently assaulting a young boy. A father of three, he was dark-haired and had a beard. Although he was the larger and stronger of the two men, it was his partner in crime, thirty-three-year-old Geoffrey Evans who came from Tyldesly in Manchester, who was the dominant one. Evans was of slight build, with blond hair, and had notched up thirty-six previous convictions, mostly for robbery. Both also had convictions for possession of heroin – a drug that had hardly even been heard of in Ireland at the time. And they were about to shatter several other taboos.

Not long after arriving in Ireland they were in trouble with the law. They appeared before Cork Circuit Court in February 1975 on sixteen counts of burglary, crimes which had been carried out over several weekends at various locations in Cork and Tipperary. They were convicted and served eighteen months in Mountjoy Jail. On their release in August 1976 they undertook a new crime spree: they decided to rape and murder one Irish woman a week.

Their first victim was twenty-three-year-old Elizabeth Plunkett. She was spending a weekend in Brittas Bay with friends, but she left the group after a row made her feel that the weekend was being spoiled. She would probably have returned to the pub if Evans had not driven up, alone, and asked her if she needed a lift home. Elizabeth made the decision that cost her her life: she accepted his offer and got into the car. Once she was in the car, Evans collected Shaw, who tied Elizabeth up on the back seat. They drove as far as Castletymon Wood, less than a mile from McDaniel's pub, and repeatedly raped her. According to his later statement, Evans then instructed Shaw to kill Elizabeth, warning: 'Remember what happened in England.' Shaw strangled her with a shirtsleeve. They left her badly beaten body in the woods that night.

As career criminals, the men had learned about the potential of forensic evidence the hard way – through courtroom battles. Now they set about destroying all links between themselves and Elizabeth Plunkett. This time around they were determined not to leave the trail of evidence that had characterised their crime scenes in Britain.

The following night they returned to Castletymon Wood, retrieved Elizabeth's body and brought it down to the beach. They stole a boat and dumped the body in the Irish Sea, anchoring it to the seabed with a stolen lawnmower. The next day they got rid of her clothes and possessions by burning them on a pyre in a caravan park. A concerned member of the public called the police, but when questioned the pair gave false names – John and Geoffrey Murphy – and although they were physically very different, they told gardaí they were brothers. They claimed the fire was to burn their own clothes, which they said had been destroyed in heavy rain. They got off with a warning to move on. Nobody at this stage connected the missing person's report on Elizabeth Plunkett to the burning of clothes in the caravan park. As a result, their debased plan to rape and murder one Irish woman a week continued unchecked.

Shaw and Evans criss-crossed the country over the next month, carrying out a spate of burglaries on the way. Aside from the houses and pubs they hit, they also robbed a fern-coloured Ford Cortina from Mitchelstown in County Cork and a roof-rack from Castletown in Wexford. They painted the stolen car black and headed for Clonmel, County Tipperary, where they applied for, and were granted, provisional driving licenses under the assumed names of Roy Hall and David Ball.

On 10 September they arrived in Galway and rented a caravan at a caravan park in Barna, west of the city. On 22 September they set out for Castlebar, County Mayo. They stopped *en route* for petrol in Maam Bridge, County Galway. An astute garage-owner realised that something was amiss because their vehicle looked so suspicious. The paint job on the car was poor – they had used paintbrushes instead of spray paint – and the number plates did not tally with the year of the model, and black Ford Cortinas were hardly ever seen in Galway. His suspicions were backed by the fact that he had heard the news reports about two wanted Englishmen, and these two seemed to fit the bill. Accordingly, he made a note of their registration number – SZH 562 – and passed it on to the local gardaí. His vigilance saved an untold number of women from a gruesome fate.

It was after dark on Wednesday, 22 September 1976 when the pair arrived in Castlebar and spotted twenty-three-year-old Mary Duffy, a slight, petite woman, weighing only seven stone, who suffered from serious spinal problems. She had just exited one phone box and was going into another.

Mary had left work just after 11pm. From 9am to 5pm she worked as a waitress and at night she was the cook in The Coffee Shop on Ellison Square. She was exhausted by the time she was due to head home and was trying to contact her brother to arrange a lift. The first phone she tried was out of order, so she went on to another. But she had no luck getting through to her brother Michael, who worked in a garage eight miles away. Michael had been sent out on a last-minute job and was late returning. When he got back he went looking for his sister on the street where he usually collected her, but couldn't find her. Michael would not see his sister alive again.

In the following days he would learn how several local people had looked out their windows upon hearing the sound of a woman 'screaming and moaning'. One witness would describe the noise as not just the sound of someone who was hurt, but specifically the sound of someone who was being hurt by someone else. Another witness heard a man shouting, 'Get in'. Only one saw a dark car reversing away at speed. On the road outside these houses gardaí would discover Mary Duffy's broken dentures – testifying to the violence of her abduction.

In the back of the car, Mary was tied up with twine and rubber and subjected to the same horror as Elizabeth Plunkett. But in Mary Duffy's case the two men decided to keep her alive for longer. They took turns getting in the back to rape her while the other drove. She was horrifically beaten and repeatedly raped over the sixty-five mile journey from the phone box where she was abducted to the men's final destination – an old railway station at Ballinahinch, 600 yards from Ballinahinch

Castle Hotel, which had been unoccupied since 1975. Mary was raped again in an area near the river, and then tied to a tree while Shaw and Evans slept in a tent nearby. She had been given five or six sleeping pills, which she readily took.

Some time within the next thirty-six hours, Mary's torturers killed her by putting a cushion over her face and suffocating her. They put her body in the boot of the car and drove to Lough Inagh, nine miles from Ballinahinch, not far from Kylemore Abbey. The lake is seventy-five feet deep in places. They broke into a boathouse and stole a boat, oars, a sledge-hammer, a cavity block and an anchor. They sailed a distance out into the lake and dumped Mary's body over the side, weighted down with the cavity block.

Four days after her kidnap, on Saturday, at 11.15pm, gardas Jim Boland and PJ Corcoran from Salthill Garda Station were passing the Ocean Wave Hotel, which faces out on the promenade. They spotted a black Cortina with the registration SZH 562. Garda Boland recognised the number as that provided by the garage-owner in Maam Bridge, along with the description of a black Cortina driven by two Englishmen who were acting suspiciously. It had to be more than just coincidence.

Boland drove his squad car out of view and radioed for immediate back-up. He had barely done so when two men came out of the hotel and got into the Cortina. The men had seen a woman walking along the promenade and were on their way to abduct her. There was no way the garda could have known this, but his quick action saved that woman from an unthinkable ordeal. He turned his headlights on and drove in front of the Cortina, blocking their path.

Garda Boland jumped out and approached the vehicle. He asked the men their names and they identified themselves as Roy Hall and David Ball. Their only verification was a receipt for the purchase of a caravan in Barna Caravan Park. The tax disc on the car had been altered. Garda Boland asked the driver, John Shaw, if he owned the car and he claimed he did. Garda Boland told Shaw that he did not, and that the car was stolen. He put his hand on Shaw's shoulder and told him he was under arrest. The men were brought in for questioning and members of the murder squad were dispatched from the Central Detective Unit (CDU) in the Phoenix Park, Dublin, to interrogate them. Shaw almost escaped by squeezing through a toilet window, but was captured after a chase. Both men – interviewed separately – denied any involvement with the missing women.

At 4am, Detective Gerry O'Carroll started to interrogate John Shaw. He learned that Shaw was a Roman Catholic and decided to try to appeal to his conscience by inviting him to recite a decade of the rosary. At the sound of the words of the prayer, Shaw began to scream and grabbed the detective by the hand. He was hallucinating – he claimed the devil had entered the room and was coming for him. And then he began to confess. Although interviews are not permitted at such hours, as suspects can claim they were deprived of sleep, the evidence was permitted because at the time, prior to Shaw's confession, the gardaí believed there was a real hope that Mary Duffy might still be alive somewhere.

Armed with Shaw's confession, detectives now knew the locations of the crime scenes and the task of gathering evidence began. In Elizabeth Plunkett's case, so much time had elapsed (over one month) that it was virtually impossible to gather any suitable forensic evidence. But Mary Duffy's case was quite different, making it doubly important that we gathered what was needed as quickly as possible.

Some scenes in my memory are frozen in time. I remember going to County Mayo that September in 1976, to the place where Mary Duffy had been subjected to such cruel and sadistic torture. In the lonely, disused grounds of the Ballinahinch Castle Hotel, that young woman met an end you and I cannot even begin to imagine. She was kept alive to gratify the warped and violent desires of two animals. Yet, as I stood there, the setting was idyllic: the lake absolutely still, mirror-like, holding a shimmering reflection of the castle against a backdrop of evergreens. I stood in a clearing and tried to understand how anyone could not, in the presence of such tranquil beauty, be jolted out of whatever rage was consuming them.

I was distracted from my thoughts when, from the corner of my eye, something incongruous made itself felt – a clump of white paper that did not belong in this scene, a reminder that all things are imperfect. I was not expecting to find anything in the way of evidence; the area had already been combed by garda technical experts. I was there purely to direct them as to the best locations to collect the samples of shingle and soil I would need to link Mary Duffy and her killers to each other and to this place. Nonetheless, I walked across and picked up the wedge of paper, still unsure that it had anything to do with the crime at all. It was a ball of toilet paper, and when I studied it, I could not believe what I had found. There was a clear and distinct impression of a row of teeth, tiny against the size of the wad of paper. It left me cold to think what kind of force the killers must have used – compared to the size of the little jaw, this was a huge gag, one which could easily have choked the victim. So not only had they tied up Mary Duffy so that she was unable to move, they had also disabled her voice in a place so remote that only their own consciences might have heard her.

The evidence was crucial: earlier, detectives had found Mary Duffy's dentures on the roadside and now I could use this for comparison. For forensic purposes, bitemarks may be divided into two categories: human on human, as on the skin during an assault; or an impression left on food, which can confirm the presence of a particular person at a particular location. One can tell immediately that a bitemark is human and not animal in origin as human impressions make an elliptical pattern, while other animals leave a v-shape indent. This wad of paper that I had found was the first trace we had of Mary. I had found traces of her rapists' semen on the seat of the car, but she had remained invisible – until now. The search for Mary Duffy's body continued. If we could locate her remains, we would have the most important link in the chain.

The garda investigation had also turned up excellent evidence. Detective Colm Dardis, attached to the Ballistics Section, went to the boathouse at Lough Inagh on 28 September and discovered a gully or crater on the roadside holding the remains of a fire. He brought the ashes back to the Lab for analysis.

The ashes were also taken from the railway site at Ballinahinch. In these I detected portions of bright red material of a fine, knitted type, which was consistent with the sweater Mary had been wearing on her last day. I also found portions of a heavier type of woollen material with a squared pattern of a reddish-purple colour intertwined with dark blue colours – her brother identified it as her distinctively patterned coat. There were also portions of burned leather and what appeared to be the high heel of a leather boot, which family members confirmed she had been wearing. There was also a fine material resembling a coat-lining.

Among the charred remains I found seven differently coloured viscose rayon fibres, which matched those taken from the back seat of the car and from the ground sheet of the tent, where the men had also raped her.

Gardaí also conducted a thorough search of the caravan park in Barna. A refuse bin was found to contain a number of burnt items, including a cosmetic bag with a small scissors, a black comb, a small jar of lipsticks and eye shadow, a red purse and rosary beads. Christine Duffy, Mary's sister, identified the make-up bag she had shared with her sister. Among the debris the remains of a handbag, a tablet jar and a pair of brown tights and panty briefs were also found.

Shaw and Evans's caravan yielded more evidence. Gardaí recovered a cushion, hair and fibres, the ground sheet of a tent and pine needles that matched samples taken from the crime scene at Ballinahinch. I was received for analysis an empty bottle labelled Dalmane – a sleeping tablet.

A tartan cushion-cover found at the railway site was of the same material and was sewn with the same thread as cushions found in the Barna caravan and in the car. A vest, T-shirt and underpants found in the caravan had seminal stains and they had viscose rayon fibres, the same as on clothing from the fire, the back seat of the car and the ground sheet. Pubic hairs found on the vest and underpants were of the same type as those found on the ground sheet and on the back seat of the car. One was Mary Duffy's.

On 1 October, I examined the black Cortina. I took a sample of its black paint coating. Inside I found a tartan cushion cover and took swabs from stains on the doors and seating. There was a lot of semen on the back seat of the car and similar samples of acid phosphates – found in large quantities in seminal fluid – were also found on the ground sheet of the tent.

There were a number of pine needles of different varieties in the debris taken from the car and these were similar to those taken from the tent site at Ballinahinch station.

A reel of white twine and some rubber tubing were found in the boot. White twine that gardaí had found on some flattened grass near the railway station at Ballinahinch matched that taken from the boot of the car. Also in the boot I found loose granules of cement, the composition of which I compared with the block that was eventually found tied to Mary's body. They matched. Neville Stewart, the caretaker at Barna House Caravan site, told Gardai he had seen Shaw and Evans put a cavity block, like the one which anchored Mary's body, into the Cortina. He had innocently presumed that the pair intended to use it to prop up their caravan.

In all, there were seven items common to the car and the disused railway site.

On 10 October the gardaí found Mary Duffy's body at the bottom of the lake. A block anchor and sledgehammer were tied around her neck, and a concrete block around her legs. She was naked and crouched in a position that was almost foetal.

The Chief State Pathologist, Professor John Harbison, conducted the post-mortem. He was satisfied from x-rays and dental records that it was her body. Gardaí had gone to her home and places of work to lift fingerprints. The prints matched those taken posthumously.

The weights were so tightly bound to her body that it took some time to free her. There were small cuts on her lips and extensive bruising all over, consistent with multiple rape. She had two black eyes. Professor Harbison found bleeding in her lungs, leading to the conclusion that she must have tried desperately to breathe and suffocated when she could not. He believed that death was due to manual strangulation, from something pressed against her face. Mary was dead when she entered the water.

From Mary Duffy's hand, Professor Harbison removed a pubic hair, which was delivered to me for analysis. On 19 October he also sent me a sample of her liver, the contents of her mouth and other material from her body, including a smear of black paint.

The hair taken from Mary Duffy's hand was the same as pubic hair found on the back seat of the Cortina and on the ground sheet of Shaw and Duffy's tent. It was not Mary Duffy's hair; it was John Shaw's hair.

Human head hair found on the right rear door of the car was the same as hair found on the ground sheet; these proved to be hairs from Mary Duffy's head – which placed her in their car.

Gardaí appealed for witnesses, to strengthen their case, and many people came forward with more pieces of the puzzle. Martin Nee, from Cashel in County Galway, stated that on 23 September he cycled to his land at Ballinahinch. He noticed the top of a tent at the rear of the disused railway station and informed the gardaí. A day or two later the tent was gone.

Patrick O'Sullivan, from Cloona, Recess, County Galway, stated that he was driving from Kylemore to Recess at 4.20am on 24 September when he saw a black Cortina – parked and with no lights on – 400 yards from the boathouse beside Lough Inagh.

Michael Staunton, the caretaker of the boathouse, stated that at 9.30am on 24 September he noticed a pane of glass was missing from the boathouse and discovered that a crook anchor and sledgehammer had been stolen.

Michael McCahill, a garage-owner from Toombeola, four miles from Roundstone, County Galway, stated that on 24 September two Englishmen in a Cortina bought £2 worth of petrol. Mr McCahill noted the car registration number because it did not correspond with the the year and model of the car.

Martin Coneally of Roundstone was in Keane's pub at Maam Cross on 24 September. At 9.15pm a dark-haired, scruffily dressed man entered, had a drink and a beef burger and watched TV for half an hour.

On 25 September, Patrick Mullen from Doonhulla saw a black Cortina coming from the Roundstone direction. The rear number plate was hanging off and appeared to be too old for the make and model of vehicle.

Michael Coneally from Clifden stated that while driving towards Clifden on 25 September, he saw two men standing on the Weir Bridge over the Ardagh river. They were dumping articles into the river, including a blue sleeping bag. A black Cortina was parked on the bridge. The sleeping bag, along with a piece of an eiderdown and a sheet, was later recovered by a garda diver.

* * *

The trials of John Shaw and Geoffrey Evans proceeded separately. The witness accounts, along with the forensic evidence, presented a strong case for the prosecution. Rex Mackey was the Senior Counsel for Shaw. He wanted to challenge the jurors before they were sworn in to find out if they had seen a recent edition of the *Late Late Show* on RTÉ television, which was held to have been in flagrant contempt by both the Supreme and High courts. An attempt was also made to hold the show's presenter, Gay Byrne, in contempt, but the court held that he was not responsible for what had been said on the show. Justice McWilliam turned down the application and said that normal citizens would treat as pure entertainment a programme they had seen on TV.

John Shaw was sentenced to life imprisonment for the murder of Mary Duffy, fourteen years for her rape and two years for kidnapping her. Geoffrey Evans got life for the murder of Mary Duffy and twenty years for the rape of Mary Duffy and Elizabeth Plunkett. The men's defence team lodged an appeal with the Supreme Court, based on the unorthodox way in which the men had been interrogated – in the middle of the night. Even after a savage double murder, it seems that accused men's rights extend to a full night's sleep, while the bereaved family's inability to rest does not come into the picture. However, Judge Griffin, who announced the ruling, found that the right to life supersedes an accused's right to the presumption of innocence: 'If a balance is to be struck between one person's right to liberty, for some hours or even days, and another person's right to protection against danger to his life, then in any civilised society in my view, the latter right must prevail.'

This case demonstrated that it is not just scientists who are learning from advances in forensic techniques, criminals too have started adapting. As new ways of linking them to their crimes are revealed, they are increasingly taking precautions to try to outwit the forensic investigators. As a result, semen is often not found in serial rape cases because the rapists know it can identify them. Shaw and Evans took steps to eradicate any forensic evidence by trying to wipe away any traces of semen from inside the car, burning the women's clothes and dumping their bodies at sea. And even in cases where the police do get a swab from semen deposited in a rape victim, they have to know where to look for its match.

PROFILING STRANGER RAPISTS

Behaviour is very individual and not something that can be easily stage-managed, and it is probably in this area that the future of forensic science lies. Behavioural patterns give very accurate clues as to an individual's personality, lifestyle and probable circumstances. This is where criminal profiling and forensic psychology come in.

TV viewers will be familiar with the techniques employed by psychologists through popular crime series such as *Cracker* and *Profiler*. But popularity does not mean workability, and there are those who are sceptical of the practice. Accordingly, a recent study by the Home Office in Britain undertook to scientifically establish whether profiling is actually of any use to detectives investigating sex crimes. Dr Anne Davis, a colleague in the Crime Analysis Unit of New Scotland Yard, examined the findings and its from her report that the following is taken.

The study was based on a group of 210 'stranger rapists', that is, men who did not know their victims before the meeting that immediately preceded the rape. The men surveyed ranged in age from fourteen to fifty-nine. The average age was twenty-seven, and three-quarters were under thirty-three years old.

Some 84 percent of the entire group had previously been in trouble with the law – the vast majority for house burglaries. Burglary was not the only crime, however – 67 percent had committed two or more sexual offences in the past, making them serial sex offenders.

The researchers found a strong correlation between the rapists' living arrangements and convictions received prior to the rape. The homeless had the highest conviction rate, followed by those in rented accommodation, while those with their own homes had committed the least number of crimes. It may be the case that men who own their own home have more to lose, or it may be the case that the homeless can 'disappear' into the woodwork more easily. It was also found that rapists who were unemployed were more likely to have criminal records than those with jobs. The relevance of this is that if the police know that the rapist they are looking for in all probability has previous convictions for burglary, it considerably narrows their search.

Behaviour that was found to be significant during a rape included the wearing of gloves. Those men who wore gloves during the attack were found to be four times more likely to be a burglar. Those who took no fingerprint precautions were approximately three times more likely to be once-off sexual offenders.

The survey found that when the rapists had used 'sighting precautions' – tried to prevent the victim from seeing his face by covering it, or by blindfolding hers – it actually indicated someone inexperienced who was preoccupied with personal safety. The rapist who had used alcohol prior to or during a rape was approximately two-and-a-half times more likely to be a one-off sexual offender, that is, less likely to be a serial rapist.

The clearest indicator that a rapist had a prior conviction for a sexual offence was if he either left no semen or attempted to destroy semen. The exhibition of forensic knowledge indicates that they are four times more likely to have prior convictions for sexual offences.

Although the study group was relatively small, the trends learned have proved to be of huge importance to police forces when narrowing down a suspect list, and building up an offender profile. Broadly, these statistics might be said to show that a person's behaviour is modified by their experience. A profile of that experience is deduced from their behaviour.

If such things had been known over thirty years before this survey was carried out, it would have led the police straight to Shaw and Evans and might have saved Mary Duffy's life. In terms of the profiling study findings, they met many of the criteria for serial rapists: they fell into the 'transient', 'burglars', 'with previous convictions' categories. Only Elizabeth Plunkett and Mary Duffy can say whether they fit into the rest.

CHAPTER 23:
THE ASSASSINATION OF
CHRISTOPHER EWART BIGGS

ON WEDNESDAY, 21 JULY 1976, the British Ambassador to Ireland, Christopher Ewart Biggs, was blown up by a 100lb car bomb, scarcely 200 yards from his official residence in Sandyford, County Dublin. There was no way he could have survived the blast. The ambassador was fifty-four years old and a father of three; his youngest child was just eight years old. His wife, Jane, heard the news of his assassination on her car radio in Fishguard, in Wales, while on a trip to visit her mother.

The following day the headlines warned that the nation's security was 'in shambles' and that the crime had 'filled all decent Irish people with a sense of shame'. I have to admit that it was a deeply humbling experience to be an Irishman on that day. Ewart Biggs had held the post for just twelve days and was on his way, with Brian Cubbon, permanent under-secretary to the Northern Ireland Office, to his first formal meeting with the Minister for Foreign Affairs, Garret FitzGerald.

Stolen deaths are always premature and therefore always doubly tragic, as a person's unfulfilled potential is lost forever. Never more so than in the case of Ewart Biggs. He could not have been more qualified for the post and the loss of his potential here was staggering. Ewart Biggs was committed to resolving the Northern crisis and to Ireland's participation in a single European community. He had a long history of service in war zones, having joined the Foreign Service in 1947 after six years as a soldier serving under Field Marshal Montgomery in North Africa; he lost an eye at El Alamein during the Second World War; and had experience in the Middle East, Algeria, Tripoli, the Persian Gulf and the Philippines. His previous posting had been in the British Embassy in Paris, and before that in Brussels, Belgium. Aside from his distinguished career in the military, he was also extremely creative. As an Oxford scholar he had written three novels, somewhat in the manner of Graham Greene, although one of his novels, *Trial by Fire*, published in 1956, had been banned in Ireland because of its love scenes.

On Tuesday 20 July, Biggs had commented to a journalist, 'Violence achieves nothing.' But just after 9.30am on the following day, all that was left of him was tangled in metal wreckage in a crater fifteen feet deep and thirty feet wide. Also killed in the blast was twenty-six-year-old London secretary Judith Cook, who worked for Brian Cubbon. Cubbon and his chauffeur, Brian O'Driscoll from Dublin, survived and recovered in intensive care in St Vincent's Hospital.

Paramedic Patrick Flood described the devastation: 'When we turned onto the road we were met by rubble and chunks of earth everywhere. The car was lying on its left-hand side, off the road, facing towards the residence. The four in it were huddled on top of each other and were all unconscious.'

Condemnation from Biggs's colleagues and friends was all-encompassing: 'I do not envy these men their consciences in their avid pursuit of hate,' said the British prime minister James Callaghan. The opposition leader, Margaret Thatcher, declared: 'We must make it clear that they will never weaken our resolve to root out terrorism by every possible means.'

Forensically, we determined that the bombers had planted the bomb under a culvert (an underground channel) that ran from the front gate of the Glencairn estate and under the adjoining Murphystown Road. A wire trailed from the bomb across fields to a plunger. The assassins had waited for the ambassador's convoy to pass, and at the first sight of his blue Jaguar car they depressed the plunger, blasting two people into eternity and maiming two others. But there the trail, and our knowledge, ended. The government offered a £20,000 reward for information – the same amount as had been offered after the murder of Garda Reynolds. But it led to nothing. Without any suspects with whom to compare evidence from the scene of the crime, we floundered.

Nobody has ever been convicted for the crime, but nobody doubted that the Provisional IRA were behind the bomb. Just before the attack, the organisation had indicated that British civil servants would be treated as legitimate targets. Another link to the IRA was suggested by the fact that the type of device used in the explosion was being used at that time almost exclusively in Northern Ireland against British soldiers.

CHAPTER 24:
TARGET: Dublin

THROUGHOUT THE LATE 1970S, tension in Northern Ireland continued to rise as sectarian tit-for-tat violence escalated. The IRA's list of 'legitimate targets' grew lengthier, and soon Dublin and London were added to it.

In 1976 there were two major sessions of firebombing in Dublin city-centre shops. The more serious batch – in terms of the threat to human life – exploded on Sunday 29 August in various pubs and cinemas. The damage caused was estimated at £750,000. A major garda alert flashed from Dublin Castle to city-centre patrol cars, warning all officers to look out for further blazes; we were in damage limitation territory. Although there was speculation that the fires were a pre-emptive strike at an emergency session of the Dáil, nobody knew where the next attack would come from.

It was imperative to find the person responsible before they had a chance to wreak yet more havoc. In this instance we did secure a prosecution, and in so doing gleaned an insight into the warped minds of those intent on mass destruction.

Vivian Patrick Hayden, with an address at Lakelands Park in Terenure, was the prime suspect. He was twenty-four years old, married and the father of a four-month-old baby, and he worked as an ESB storeman. He seemed a 'normal Joe' and a good neighbour, except he kept a copy of the IRA constitution, *Óglaigh na hÉireann*, in his flat, along with ammunition stores.

In his home gardaí found 200 cassette cases, seventeen strapless wristwatches, batteries, four gas-head lighters, a soldering iron and a jar of sodium chlorate – an explosive substance. It fell to the Lab to link these ingredients with the incendiaries planted in the pubs and cinemas.

I examined an unexploded device from the Ambassador cinema and fifteen other incendiaries, seven of which were badly burned. The intact, unexploded device was examined thoroughly. A wristwatch was glued to the bottom left-hand corner of the outside of the transparent cassette case cover. The minute and second hands of the watch had been removed and the hour hand was bent upwards. A drawing pin, placed in the 12 o'clock position, was secured to the surface of the watch by narrow pieces of sellotape. A wire was soldered to the top of the pin, the other end of which was soldered to the positive terminal of an Ever Ready battery, which was inside the cassette case, in the top left-hand corner.

A second wire was soldered to the base of the battery. This wire was attached to a small light bulb fixed inside the case in the top right-hand corner. A third wire led from the bulb to the screw attachment of a gas lighter head. A fourth wire went from the base of the gas lighter head to the body of the watch. The upper portion of the gas lighter head, which contained the heating element, was pushed through a hole in a self-seal plastic bag, which contained the explosive mixture of sugar and sodium chlorate. In the cassette case there was also a lighter fuel container, holding petrol, an explosive and flammable liquid.

It was very rudimentary, but it worked. When the hour hand of the watch rotated and touched the drawing pin – that is, when it struck twelve – an electrical circuit would be completed; a current would pass, heating the element in the gas lighter head, which would, in turn, detonate the sugar/chlorate mixture. The resulting fire would be aided by the presence of the petrol.

In each of the sixteen devices, I found that the hour hand of the watch had been bent upwards in the same S shape, suggesting that they were all of common origin. They were all primed to go off at midnight, also suggesting a connection. I compared the devices with objects found in the defendant's flat. Every component, except for a type of bulb, was found there – right down to the brands of batteries and watches chosen – and I thought it reasonable, therefore, to assume the devices had been made there.

Hayden's fingerprint was found on a piece of adhesive tape on the unexploded device recovered from the Ambassador cinema. The yellow and black wire used in making the bombs was of the same colour, thickness and plastic composition as wire found in Hayden's flat. The solder found in the flat was compared to the soldering on the devices and found to contain the same metallic composition. Based on this evidence, Hayden was charged and his trial was scheduled for the Special Criminal Court.

In court, Hayden's defence team maintained that all of the items found in the flat were widely available in shops and therefore in the possession of many people, and further that the S-bend of the hour hand on the watches was not unique, as it was used in other incendiary devices and was therefore was a technique common to many bomb makers. They put it to me that it could have been an unfortunate series of coincidences. I declared that this was highly unlikely.

Gardaí had asked Hayden what he needed the batteries for, and he replied 'a radio', but the batteries did not fit any of the radios in his possession. He said that the cassette holders were for a tape recorder – but that he had not yet bought it.

The defendant further undermined his case when he testified that he was proud to be a member of the IRA, stating that he believed in a thirty-two-county socialist, democratic, united Ireland. He admitted that he knew the devices were being made in his flat, but he claimed that they were made by a group of men from Northern Ireland whose names he refused to supply. He claimed that he had given permission for his flat to be used for making incendiary devices 'for the purpose of using in the North against the occupying forces of the Crown'. But, he said, he never intended the devices to be used in the South and was 'disgusted' when they were because 'there is no armed struggle in the South'. He was 'disappointed' and 'disgusted' when the incendiaries went off in Dublin because he did not like to see 'our beautiful city in flames'.

His line of defence was that he could not be held criminally responsible, since the devices were used for purposes other than he intended. It was a clever legal strategy because *mens rea*

– the accused's direct and specific intention – can often provide a loophole in law.

But the prosecution retaliated by asking Hayden why it did not matter to him that the devices could be used to burn, kill or maim as long as it was not in the South? Would he have been willing to take a more active part in Derry or Belfast? Would he, for instance, have actually planted the devices?

Eventually the court held that even if Hayden did not intend the incendiaries to be used in the Republic, the fact that he did intend them to be used for a similar crime of a similar nature made him criminally liable. Geography was not the issue; intention and participation were the issues.

In delivering sentence in November 1976, Mr Justice Denis Pringle said he was satisfied all the incendiary devices that had started the fires were similar in nature and had been timed to go off at midnight on the night of the bombings. Hayden got twelve years for setting fire to the Adelphi and Carlton cinemas; the Abbey Mooney, Parnell Mooney and Suffolk bars. He was also found guilty of attempting to set fire to the Ambassador cinema, the Earl Mooney and Harp bars.

CHAPTER 25: BODY IN THE LIFFEY

WHEN SOMEBODY JUST DISAPPEARS, the main problem is simply not knowing what happened. But having said that, human bodies are particularly difficult to dispose of. I recall the murder, in May 1976, of Patrick Hyland at 15b Sean McDermott Street, Dublin. His killer attempted to shove him feet first into the fire, presumably hoping it would gradually consume all of him and only ash would remain. When that inevitably failed to work, he dismembered Hyland and dumped him into the River Liffey.

A mother and her child were walking along Eden Quay when the child said he could see a hand. When the woman looked to where her son was pointing, she too recognised that the object was of human origin, but could not say for sure what it was. The body part turned out to be a human pelvis displaying sawmarks.

Dr John Harbison analysed the dismembered chunks of flesh to see if the killer had anatomical knowledge – expertise in cutting technique would have suggested the killer might be a doctor or a butcher. But he deduced instead that the killer was a fitter because the type of weapon used to cut up the limbs had the jagged edge of a hacksaw. I linked him to the crime scenes at the flat and at the river, not least by the presence of a specific industrial strength detergent in the flat and on the body but also by the cross-transfer of fibres.

CHAPTER 26:
THE DISAPPEARANCE OF
ROBERT NAIRAC

THE THIRD EVER MURDER CASE IN THE REPUBLIC to go to trial without a body involved the killing of Captain Robert Laurence Nairac.

Nairac was a British SAS officer who had gone undercover to gather information on the IRA in South Armagh. His background was very different to that of the men he now had to convince of his Republican credentials: he had attended an English public school, read history in Oxford and served with the British Army in Kenya before taking up his special assignment to Northern Ireland in 1976. The SAS motto may be 'who dares wins' and they may be one of the deadliest armies in the world, but Nairac was playing a dangerous game – one wrong move and he was most definitely out.

On 14 May 1977, at around 10pm, Nairac left the base in Bessbrook, South Armagh to go 'on duty'. He was due to return at 11.30pm. He was dressed in civilian clothing and driving a red Triumph car, the property of the Ministry of Defence. He was carrying a specially adapted Browning pistol with fifty rounds of ammunition. He went to the Three Steps Inn public house in Drumintee, South Armagh, three miles north of the border.

Inside the bar, Nairac made the fatal mistake of introducing himself as a Provo to a local woman: the Provo community is tight-knit, so new faces are greeted warily. Some reports say that other Republican customers became suspicious because he visited the loo a number of times.

After a while, Nairac got up and left the bar, heading for his car. But he only got as far as the car park when he was attacked by a gang of men. When his gun and fake driving license were discovered, he was beaten and they demanded to know who he was, accusing him of being a member of the SAS. Nairac claimed he was a 'stickie from Belfast', but this made his attackers even more suspicious – he had told the woman he was a Provo, but a stickie belongs to the opposing faction, the Official IRA. The gang asked him to give the names of 'stickies' from the area, but he couldn't. His fate was sealed.

Captain Nairac was taken to a field on the banks of Flurry River in Ravensdale, just south of the border in Dundalk. He was beaten and tortured. A gun was held to his head. The gun wasn't working and required a new magazine before it discharged – prolonging his suffering. Captain Nairac was shot in the head. His attackers then left the scene. Three of them changed their clothes and dumped their original clothing.

When Nairac's superiors discovered he had not returned on time, they were immediately on the scene. The red Triumph was still there, but the wing mirror was broken. They found two bullets, a small sum of money near the riverbank, a sweater with clumps of hair in the armpits and dried blood stains on the grass. Two shirt buttons were found with the thread still attached, indicating that they had been ripped off. Taken all together, the scene painted a picture of violence.

As he had disappeared while in the Republic, the investigation was the responsibility of the gardaí and the Irish forensic team. I requested that Captain Nairac's hairbrush be delivered from the barracks. I was able to match hairs from the brush to hairs found at the scene, so we knew for certain that it was Captain Nairac who had been accosted and abducted.

Two members of the gang fled to the USA immediately after the killing. A number of others were charged. One, Liam Patrick Townson, a twenty-four-year-old carpenter living in Louth but originally from Meigh, South Armagh, admitted to being the trigger man. He blamed alcohol for his actions. Although his evidence confirmed what was already feared – that Nairac was dead – he did not know what had happened to the body after the murder. Local folklore had it that Nairac was put through an industrial shredder and that was why no trace of him could be found.

The trial proceeded without the body and Townson was sentenced to life in the Special Criminal Court in 1977. Life in his case meant twelve years. Four others were convicted in Belfast.

CHAPTER 27:
THE MOUNTBATTEN MURDERS

MODERN SOCIETIES ARE MOULDED BY the atrocities they have endured. Following the murders of the British ambassador, Christopher Ewart Biggs and Queen Elizabeth's cousin, Lord Mountbatten, I believe a line was crossed and there was no going back. The country was left with a feeling that nothing was sacred anymore, that no one was safe. The threat posed to the security of the State following the murder of seventy-nine-year-old Lord Mountbatten on 27 August 1979 was unprecedented.

In 1979 the north of Ireland was divided by sectarianism. The Protestant and Catholic communities were suspicious of one another and violence was rife. The Provisional IRA was continually upping the ante in its efforts to force the British out of Ireland. Against this backdrop, the IRA struck where they knew it would hurt the British Empire most: Lord Mountbatten was the great-grandson of Queen Victoria, a cousin of Queen Elizabeth, a favourite 'uncle' of Prince Charles and a nephew of the last Tsarina of Russia.

Lord Mountbatten was a creature of habit and it was this that proved to be his downfall. Routine is what assassins depend on – it allows them to predict the movements of their subject and plan their moves to the second. So it was with Mountbatten. He holidayed at the family's summer retreat, Classiebawn Castle in Mullaghmore, eight miles from Sligo, every year.

Mountbatten may have been a creature of habit, but he was not ignorant of the threat posed by the IRA. At the outset of the Troubles, around 1971, he had expressed concerns about his personal security to the British cabinet, but experts from the Home Office, Foreign Office and Ministry of Defence advised him in a memo: 'No one can say that there is no risk in any visit to Ireland in present circumstances. Nevertheless they all feel that the risk is one which can reasonably be taken.' The castle at Classiebawn was under guard, but Lord Mountbatten never allowed security men aboard his twenty-seven-foot-long boat. Perhaps collecting lobster pots in the company of armed detectives while holidaying in a sleepy harbour village seemed incongruous.

On 27 August 1979, at 11.30am, Lord Mountbatten set out from Mullaghmore harbour, Sligo, with his daughter and her husband, Lord and Lady Brabourne, their twin sons Timothy and Nicholas (fourteen years old), the twins' grandmother, Dowager Lady Brabourne and a fifteen-year-old local boy, Paul Maxwell, taken along to steer the boat. On 28 August the State pathologist Dr John Harbison and I were gazing down at four of these people in the morgue.

Those who witnessed the explosion that morning remember most vividly the screams of the survivors. We would later discover that the device that blew the boat apart contained 15lb of gelignite and was probably detonated from nearby cliffs by remote control, using radio signals.

The first body we examined was Mountbatten's grandson, Nicholas, who had been killed instantly. His twin, Timothy, was badly injured but had survived. However, almost every part of his body had sustained injuries – typical in a bombing. He was blinded in one eye and deafened in one ear and had to undergo an operation for a suspected burst spleen. But most devastating for him was the loss of his brother, with whom he had shared a room since birth. The boys' mother and father had also miraculously survived. Dowager Lady Brabourne was the second body; she died on 28 August from her injuries.

Paul Maxwell was the third fatality. He was on the last day of a summer holiday job and just happened to be in the wrong place at the wrong time. Paul's body was extremely badly damaged, blown apart in the upper stomach and chest area. There were many pieces of wood protruding from his wounds. The sight of the boat's layers of green and white paint driven into his chest was pathetic. But forensically it was important, as it indicated that the explosion must have taken place behind a green-and-white painted wooden structure. I knew from the tattering of their clothing, Mountbatten's shattered legs and the way the flesh had been stripped away from the limbs on all three bodies that they had been very near to the explosive when it detonated. All of these things indicated that the bomb had been on the boat; they never stood a chance.

The final body was that of Lord Mountbatten. He was one of the most dignified corpses I have ever seen in my life. For those not used dealing with the dead I should probably qualify that statement – I mean that death seemed unable to diminish the man's dignity. Usually with murder victims there is no sense of repose, because of the agony of their final moments. One can see, etched into their faces, the realisation that life is being violently stolen from them. But Lord Louis Albert Francis Victor Nicholas Mountbatten, or 'Dickie' as he was known to his friends, was different; one could say defiant. Looking upon his corpse, I got the sense that nothing they could do to him could take away what he had achieved in his lifetime.

In the Second World War he had been a senior naval officer in the British Army. He had saved his entire crew when his destroyer, *HMS Kelly*, was torpedoed by the Germans in the Mediterranean off the coast of Malta in 1941. He held Burma from the Japanese towards the end of the war, and he was Viceroy of India when, following a sustained campaign of both violent uprising and passive resistance, the British handed the country back to the Indian people in 1947. In life he was a man of ability, passion and intelligence. Laid out in the morgue at Sligo General Hospital, his remarkable, eagle-like profile – running from the bones over his eyes to his aquiline nose and huge jutting chin – was still fierce and intact. He was seventy-nine years old and the victim of an assassination, but he still had that distinctive masculine profile and everything about him seemed in harmony.

The outrage that followed the murder was international. Flags were flown at half-mast in India, and schools and government offices closed for a week as a mark of respect. Burma declared three days of national mourning. But, as bad as the atrocity was, it was about to get worse. On the very same day, the IRA killed eighteen British soldiers at Warrenpoint, County Down.

The IRA showed no remorse for the carnage. The *Republican News* described the bombing of Mountbatten's boat as a 'discriminate operation to bring to the attention of the English people the continuing occupation of our country. We will tear out their sentimental imperialist heart. The execution was a way of bringing emotionally home to the English ruling class and its working class slaves that their government's war on us is going to cost them as well.'

The words seem incredibly inhumane when compared to those of the victims and survivors. Timothy Knatchbull learned about his twin's death while he himself was being treated in hospital: 'I knew in the first minute that this was so calamitous for me that I must either get over it in that minute or I would never get over it. We had not spent more than five days apart during fifteen (*sic*) years.' Years later, Timothy set up a support group for twins who had been bereaved.

A friend of Paul Maxwell described the pitiful way in which a fifteen-year-old boy had become a 'legitimate target': 'He always loved going out on trips on board Lord Mountbatten's boat when he was on holiday here before. This year Mountbatten was looking for someone to help maintain the boat and take it out for runs every day. Paul was very happy at the job and was down at the quay every day getting it ready for the outings.' A commemorative plaque was placed in the chapel of Paul's school. It bears the words of the 107th Psalm: *They that go down to the sea in ships and occupy their business in great waters: these men see the works of the Lord and his wonders in the deep.*

Paul Maxwell's father, John, who had played rugby for Ulster, witnessed the explosion and the aftermath: 'I was on the harbour-side and knew the boat had just gone out when I heard the explosion. I jumped in the car to get to a spot where I could see more clearly, and when I got there I knew my son was dead. I could not believe that anybody survived such an explosion. There was little left of the boat apart from debris floating on the surface. I knew he was gone. He was a better Irishman than those who did that foul deed.' John Maxwell later helped found an integrated school in Enniskillen, County Fermanagh.

Despite the horror of the event and the widespread outrage and disgust at such a barbarous act, the story might well have ended there, without the bombers ever being brought to justice, had it not been for sheer chance. Before the bomb had even gone off, at 9.40am, two men had been stopped at a routine checkpoint a few miles from Granard, County Longford. The driver identified himself as Patrick Rehill, but had no identification. He was acting so suspiciously that the garda asked him to recite the car's registration number. He was unable to do so. The passenger identified himself as Thomas McMahon, a known IRA man and explosives expert. The pair were brought in for questioning.

At Granard station a garda recognised the man using the alias Patrick Rehill. His real name was Francis McGirl and he was a Republican sympathiser. The men were immediately arrested under the Offences Against the State Act.

During interrogation, McGirl cracked and blurted out: 'I put no bomb on the boat.' The interviewing gardaí could only ask what he was talking about. 'No answer,' replied McGirl. But later, when it was learned that a bomb had detonated, it was too big a coincidence to ignore.

Scant though it was, that was all we had to go on: the blabbering of a panicked man. It fell to me to either link McGirl and McMahon to the crime scene, or to eliminate them from the investigation. Gardaí brought me the suspects' clothing and shoes, as well as the mats from the car in which they had been travelling when stopped. The remnants of the victims' clothing were removed from the bodies and also sent to me. Among the items were Mountbatten's vest and his dark blue sweater. Nicholas's clothing had his nametag on it – a common practice for boarding-school pupils. Among the debris they retrieved from the water were fragments of the boat, and pieces of wood and paint.

The Lab tests were laborious but extremely damning. On Lord Mountbatten's sweater and on a piece of wood from the boat I found nitroglycerine – a component of gelignite. There were also traces of nitroglycerine on the clothing of Thomas McMahon.

I found sand in the mats from the suspects' car, on their clothes and in their shoes. I immediately requested gardaí to collect samples of the sand at Mullaghmore Harbour, from around the tidal area where *Shadow V* had been moored, from the sand dunes and from the seabed where the debris of the boat lay. Granules of sand are highly distinctive when magnified 300 times under the electron microscope and, sure enough, I found that the sand from the suspects' shoes and car mat matched that from Mullaghmore beach. There was a lot of sea sand on Thomas McMahon's shoes and socks. By 'a lot' I mean that the sand was plainly visible and encrusted about the boots, inside and outside. Since sand loosens and falls away quite quickly, I deduced it must have been fairly recently acquired, which, if they were guilty, would be consistent with the mens' early apprehension.

I compared the sand from McMahon's shoes to control samples taken from a huge variety of coastlines and from other locations inland – locations that had no relevance to the crime scene. No such study of similarities or differences in sand had ever been undertaken before, but I reasoned that forensics would not fail me. After all, granules of pollen taken from the Turin Shroud – the holy cloth that Roman Catholics believe was used to wrap the body of Jesus Christ in the tomb – have been analysed by forensic experts and successfully dated to the time of his crucifixion. In contrast, my particular study did not have to date the grains, only compare them. Even so, I was amazed at the complex differences I found between the grains of sand taken from the crime scene and the control samples. First, I identified the Mullaghmore samples as being sea sand because they were rounded – consistent with the rolling effect of waves and tidal action. I found the control samples of building sand and lake sand to be 'sharp' in comparison. In composition, the sea sand contained traces of sodium chloride, or sea salt, fragments of seashells and tiny coloured stones.

The sand on McMahon's boots and stockings was the same as sand taken from near where the boat lay in the bay, but it differed from all other control samples. I individualised it by its appearance, its components and the fragments of shell and stone. Although it would be rare to get sand that was unique to a specific beach, the probability of the sand from any two stretches of coastline being the same was extremely slight.

I then turned my attention to the evidence offered by the four victims. The paint flakes from the body of Paul Maxwell consisted of two types: the first a type white paint and the other consisting of two different types of green paint, a dark green top layer and lime green undercoat. Mountbatten had been superstitious when it came to green paint. He believed it was a lucky colour ever since he had saved his crew from *HMS Kelly* – a green boat. He insisted that his fishing boat was always painted green, and this apparently irrelevant fact was singularly important in linking his killers to the crime scene.

As soon as I saw green flecks of paint on Thomas McMahon's boots, I was visited by a flashback of Paul Maxwell's open chest covered in paint chips of exactly the same colour. It was damning evidence, made even more damning when similar flecks were also found in the front passenger seat of the men's car. The flecks from the car also consisted of two layers of green paint, one dark green and the other lime green. The colours of the flecks were exactly the same as those of the paint which had practically held Mountbatten's ten-year-old fishing boat together. This paint was found on all of the bodies and on McMahon's jacket as well as his boots. The dark green paint was Interlux Yacht enamel, colour number 995. I calculated the probability of McMahon otherwise coming into contact with paint flakes having the same composition, shade and exactly the same layers as being 250,000 to one.

The accumulated forensic evidence was enough to have McMahon and McGirl charged with murder.

The Mountbatten Trial:
The First Attempt on My Life

It was during the subsequent trial that the first attempt was made on my life. At that time I was not unused to intimidation. Frequently after court appearances I was aware that I was being followed. In 1978, during a case in the Special Criminal Court, the phone would ring in the small hours of the morning, always between one and four, and on most days of the week. Whoever was on the other end of the line would not speak. He was just letting us know how close he was and how easily he could get to us. It upset my wife considerably. However, as I was on call to the gardaí, I could not take the receiver off the hook.

Then came the night during the Mountbatten trial when the threat was so real that I truly believed my evidence would cost me my life. I had left work at about 7pm, two days before I was due to give evidence in court. As the ongoing Mountbatten case had such a high public profile, nobody was taking any chances, so I was under protection and accompanied by a garda.

I drove my car out of garda headquarters in the Phoenix Park, and immediately a very large car began to follow us, practically latching itself on to the rear bumper of my car. The driver behind was letting us know not only that he was there, but that he wanted us to know he was there. I took some detours, and when that didn't lose them the garda with me took out his revolver and held it up so that the silhouette could be seen in the driver's headlights. When the sight of the revolver did not deter them, we knew that they had come prepared and were armed.

We drove around like that for some time, absolutely terrified. I couldn't think of any place that I could drive into safely where they wouldn't open fire on me. After quite a long tour of Dublin, I felt I could not run from death any more. This was it. They had worn me down. What I can only describe as an air of surreal practicality took over. I began to think that if I were going to die, it would be preferable to die at home. That way my wife would be there and wouldn't have to get the news at second hand. And I knew I wanted her to be the one who would prepare me for my funeral, who would wash my corpse and lay me out. I also wanted her to be the one to break the news to my sisters.

As I drove into the driveway of our house, my fear was so great that the hair was literally standing up on the back of my head. I stopped the car and turned off the engine. Neither the garda nor myself knew what to expect next, or how death would come. The other car was just at the end of my drive, a few feet away. They were waiting too. I didn't get out of the car. If they were going to kill me, I was not going to initiate events and make things easy for them. Suddenly the other car reversed at high speed right out of our cul-de-sac and drove away. We were left almost with a feeling of deflation, so high were our adrenaline levels. I had thought that I was at death's door, because they seemed so intent on murder and they could so easily have achieved it. Instead I was left wondering what would happen next. Would they try again?

In any event, the forensic evidence was enough to ensure that McMahon, who had been in the IRA since he was eighteen years old, got life imprisonment for murder. McGirl was cleared of the charge as there was insufficient forensic evidence. The case against McGirl hinged on his confession while in custody, but as his only words were 'I put no bomb on the boat', the judge deemed it did not qualify as a confession of murder – McGirl had never indicated which boat he was referring to, therefore there was reasonable doubt concerning his involvement.

In 1985, McMahon was part of a mass breakout attempt at Portlaoise jail. He made headlines again in 1988 when he won a £4,000 compensation award in the Four Courts after suffering a broken arm during a strip search, but tried to escape during the compensation hearing by firing a gun. In 1998 McMahon was released under the terms of the Good Friday Agreement, by which time he had become the longest-serving Republican prisoner in an Irish jail.

CHAPTER 28: ARMED AND DANGEROUS
The Bank Robbers

AFTER THE ASSASSINATION OF LORD MOUNTBATTEN in 1979, the South became a totally different society, very much influenced by the killing and violence in Northern Ireland and the sudden availability of guns and ammunition. Crime developed a new degree of viciousness and ruthlessness as the terrorist groups began carrying out more frequent armed robberies to support their activities.

From 1976 on, the battle to preserve the State from the hands of the subversives was being lost. The fanatical offshoots springing from Republican fundamentalism, such as the Prisoners' Revenge Group (PRG) and Saor Éire, were an indication of just how healthy the movement was. The Prisoners' Revenge Group concentrated on setting fire to the cars and homes of officers associated with the Curragh prison, and our job was to link evidence from the homes back to suspects. The Garda Golf Club in Stackstown in the Dublin Mountains was also hit a number of times by the group. The PRG didn't last long, but it created a simmering fear and the lid was always threatening to blow. There were riots in prisons in support of the group, and the gardaí seized a lot of suspected explosive substances, which came to me for analysis.

In contrast, Saor Éire – which included members of both the Official and the Provisional IRA – was more criminal than political in make-up. I clearly remember one of its members who was charged, in March 1976, with painting slogans in St Mullen's Church in Graiguenamanagh, smashing up Marian shrines and urinating in public. For me, he summed up what I felt the movement was about – anti-anything for the sake of it.

The group gained the distinction of being the first organised band of armed robbers in the country, focusing particularly on financial institutions and generally timing their raids to coincide with pay-day. They had hit Dublin and Kells in County Meath quite badly in 1969, and had achieved notoriety in February 1970 when members took over the village of Rathdrum, County Wicklow: they felt so immune from the law that they cut telephone wires and held up traffic, in broad daylight, while raiding the local Hibernian Bank.

Saor Éire could have become something much more sinister, but an accident led to their premature demise. The founder, Liam Walsh, blew himself to kingdom come while transporting explosives in 1970, and without his leadership the movement floundered. The end came quickly for them after the murder of Garda Dick Fallon in Dublin, on April 3 1970. He was the first garda to be killed in the course of duty in almost three decades, and the first to die in the modern Troubles.

The gang had just raided the Royal Bank of Ireland on Arran Quay. Garda Richard Fallon and Garda Paul Firth were two of the first officers on the scene. They arrived as the gang came racing out through the door of the bank, all armed with revolvers. Gardaí Fallon and Firth gave chase and shots were fired. Garda Fallon was shot in the head.

Garda Richard Fallon was just forty-three years old and a father of five. He was one of four Fallon brothers who had joined the Force. His father, Michael, who had been a member of the 'Old' IRA, described his son as 'fearless'. Speaking to *The Irish Times* after his son's murder, he said: 'That's why he was killed. It's a great disgrace that he was not armed. He was in the LDF [FCA] before he joined the guards and he had an excellent shot.' A Special Branch officer commented: 'The honeymoon is now over. One of our men has been killed, a father of five who never did any harm to anybody. We've always been painted as the villains, the ones who are brutal. You go up and ask Dick Fallon's widow today who are the brutal ones.'

The gardaí came under increasing pressure throughout the 1980s to get the criminals under control. There emerged an international crime trade in guns and drugs, and the Irish crime bosses wanted in. In order to fund their purchases, they carried out armed robberies: in 1986, we recorded a 40 percent hike in armed offences, up to 616 from 440 the previous year.

The gardaí were now thinking in terms of what forensic science could do for them and as a result the Garda Armed Robbery Correlation Programme (GARCP) was established. The proposed task of the programme was to search for a common thread running through different armed robberies to assess – either by *modus operandi* or by trace evidence left at crime scenes – whether or not the same group of people was carrying them out.

The Garda Armed Robbery Correlation Programme was an innovative piece of policing, ahead of its time, and pre-empted many similar programmes set up by the FBI in America, including a forged documents bank, a weapons bank and even a ransom note bank.

Forensic evidence can often be the gardaí's greatest weapon against criminals, as in the case of the armed robbery of Ballyfermot post office, which resulted in the postmaster being shot and injured. Two individuals were linked to getaway cars through fibres and paint flecks, and linked to the actual scene of the crime – the post office – when we found, on their persons, the presence of a glue-like substance. It was a sealing wax, and was quite specific to the post office trade, for obvious reasons.

On other occasions, the gardaí do not require our help at all. When Ford's in Cork was robbed, the raiders chose an ingenious getaway vehicle – a dinghy – which they had hired specially for the job. The raiders held up the staff and robbed the wages, and then made good their escape in their dinghy, via Mahon. Things were going swimmingly until the thieves decided to stop off at the boathouse where they had hired their transport to recoup their deposit. Inevitably, they were caught. Some people are excessively mean!

Despite the antics of some raiders, armed robbery is an extremely dangerous and disturbing crime. If something should go wrong, you have a group of panicked men with loaded guns, and anything can happen. A good example of how things can go horribly and fatally wrong is the robbery of the Bank of Ireland in Athy, County Kildare, on 12 January 1990.

A major five-men gang, already responsible for up to a dozen armed bank robberies in provincial towns, was the focus of a four-month investigation by a Special Branch undercover team, which had tracked the gang to the Athy heist and prepared to launch a pre-emptive strike. Detectives staked out the bank premises from a local fire station, and members of the Emergency Response Unit waited in trucks. When the siege began in Emily Square, the ensuing shoot-out left two bank officials, a bystander, three detectives and two raiders injured, and a criminal dead. The siege lasted ninety minutes and two gardaí had lucky escapes.

The dead man was twenty-six-year-old Austin Higgins, a father of two from Donaghmede in Dublin. He was shot in the eye. The gang leader, who was a Provo activist from Tyrone, was wanted for questioning by the RUC in Northern Ireland. He too received gunshot wounds to the head. A bank official being held hostage was shot in the spine, and another bystander got a bullet in the leg.

The country was shocked when it heard about the showdown and public debate raged concerning the role of the gardaí in the incident. If you will excuse the pun, the gardaí were coming under fire from all sides. Ballistics had the job of examining the bullets to establish which weapon had fired which bullet. Somehow it was considered acceptable for the gardaí to have been shot by raiders' bullets, but not the other way around. Similarly, the public needed to hear that the bullets which hit bystanders were fired by raiders, not gardaí.

Here again, the 'yes but-ers' in society wanted everything their own way and were not prepared to accept that /violent delights have violent ends': terrorists cannot have it all their own way. A garda is trained to shoot at someone who puts his/her life or his/her colleagues' lives at risk. But the general public remained unconvinced. That same year the amendment removing capital punishment for the murder of a garda came into effect, despite huge opposition from the Garda Representative Authority (GRA).

However the public might have perceived it, the incident in Athy seemed to put manners on the armed-robber fraternity. They had been having it all their own way, particularly as small towns did not have armed gardaí readily available. However, the decisive action of the gardaí at Athy sent out the message that they were very serious about cracking down on crime. It certainly curbed the spate of attacks which had plagued the late 1980s.

CHAPTER 29: JAMES LYNAGH
Ritual Killer

> *'Violence created violence. Sectarian killings*
> *... illustrated just how true that was and how*
> *depraved people had become ...'*
> William Craig

SOME MEN ARE MONSTERS AND IT IS NECESSARY to label them as such. Each generation must face its own nightmare in a confrontation that leads it to create moral absolutes that will define the limits of civilisation. Today, it is paedophiles. In the 1980s, it was terrorists. One of the worst among that group of fanatics was James Lynagh, a member of the East Tyrone brigade of the IRA.

James Lynagh murdered thirty-eight people in cold blood; not one of his victims was shown any mercy. Yet society cannot condemn him as a serial killer because, in legal terms, crimes committed in the name of sectarian organisations do not fall into this category. I find this extraordinary, especially when one considers it is highly plausible that some men who are driven by a compulsion to kill will join sectarian groups simply to sate their bloodlust.

I fail to grasp why someone who kills out of a conviction of revenge should earn the mantle 'assassin', and be considered to have carried out a lesser sin than the random killer, even if he has killed far more people. Nothing can bring the dead back. Degrees of depravity should be measured only in terms of the numbers of dead and the suffering inflicted before death, not the reason for their dying.

In forensic terms, Lynagh was a ritualistic killer: his killings bore a trademark as specific to him as a signature at the bottom of a painting. Once he had executed his chosen victim in cold blood, Lynagh would riddle the corpse with bullets, pulverising human flesh beyond recognition. And yet the dead cannot suffer. A sadist requires the suffering of a living victim for gratification, so if James Lynagh was not a sadist, what was he? There is no word for a man who believes he has power over the dead, except possibly 'morally insane', or just plain 'evil'.

Lynagh was one of twelve children. The family lived in Tully, a village near Monaghan town. His criminal career started early: at just seventeen years old he began a five-year sentence in Long Kesh prison for possession of explosives. The explosives had detonated while he was transporting them, and his inner legs and upper thighs were badly maimed as a result. This affliction might partly explain his boundless, homicidal rage.

Nonetheless, the young Lynagh had popular support, and on his release from prison he was elected to the Monaghan Urban District Council. The mask of respectability could not completely obscure his true nature. In 1980, Lynagh was arrested again and charged with membership of the IRA. This time the Special Criminal Court acquitted him. But Lynagh was fast becoming a dangerous and cruel man, and he was well on his way to becoming a murderer.

Between 1981 and 1987 he engaged in a sickening killing spree perpetrated in the name of ethnic cleansing. He set out to murder the eldest sons of Protestant farmers along the border so that they could not inherit the land. Presumably, his justification was that his victims constituted 'legitimate targets'. But you can only go on for so long before you get caught.

On 6 March 1980 Henry Livingstone was heading off to feed calves in an outfield at his mother's farm in Cortynan, Tynan, County Armagh when he was murdered in cold blood. He had been looking after his elderly mother and the family farm since his father's death. He was a retired part-time UDR man, and he had been a member of the Second County Armagh Battalion. He was thirty six years old and 6ft 4ins tall: a strong man who suffered from no natural diseases which would have accelerated his death. His beliefs, however, were less conducive to good health: Livingston was a member of the Killylea True Blues Orange Lodge.

There were warning signs to suggest he was in danger, had he chosen to acknowledge them. Just under a year previously, on Good Friday 1979, his neighbour Thomas Armstrong had been killed in a sectarian attack. The circumstances of Livingstone's death were to be a carbon copy of the fate that befell his neighbour. Armstrong had been returning from feeding stock on Lord Caledon's estate – 500 yards from the border – when he was murdered. He was also a member of the UDR, which he had joined at its inception. He was older than Livingstone – sixty-four years of age – and was killed a week before he was due to retire. He too was a member of an Orange Lodge – the Cavenpole Purple Star.

Livingstone's contacts in the security forces probably briefed him that his neighbour's death bore all the hallmarks of Lynagh's handiwork. The IRA hitman's capacity for enjoying his blood-letting was fast becoming legendary. In Armstrong's case, he fired a total of fifteen bullets, two of which struck the victim in the back.

But if his neighbour's murder caused Livingstone to worry about his own safety, he had no plans to leave his home. At 12.30pm on his last day, dressed casually in a blue anorak, purple pullover, blue jeans and a pair of wellies, he went to feed the calves, as usual. Lynagh and two accomplices were lying in wait behind a stack of hay, and Lynagh opened fire as Livingstone approached the open-sided barn. The bag of meal Livingstone was carrying fell to the ground at his feet. He was killed instantly, but Lynagh was far from finished.

In all, the dead man sustained bullet wounds to the chest, six to his abdomen, two to his right leg and one to his right buttock. His spleen was completely pulped, his right kidney lacerated. There were several exit wounds, indicating just how close the gunman had been to his unsuspecting victim. The bullets were small calibre, high velocity – designed for maximum damage at point-blank range.

The number of bullets fired posthumously into Henry Livingstone's body left no doubt in the minds of experienced detectives that James Lynagh was behind the attack. The suspicion was backed up by intelligence relayed by RUC 'moles', which quickly pointed the finger of suspicion at James Lynagh. The gardaí arrested him on the same afternoon, along with two other suspects who would also be charged. But it would take more than the word of the others to convince the Special Criminal Court that an individual's behaviour and habits are as predictable as a science.

Thankfully, we were fortunate to have good detectives working on the case. The RUC moved quickly to protect the crime scene. The officer who is first on the scene of a crime must make split-second decisions on detecting, preserving and collecting evidence. Carelessness at the outset makes the scientist's role useless at the end of the process. Nothing at a crime scene can be moved or touched until it has been cordoned off and photographed. Scientists occasionally make mistakes and evidence can be destroyed on handling, or sometimes in testing. But good photographs provide a permanent overall picture of the events preceding the attack. They show the world from the distorted perspective of the criminal. The photos taken at the Livingstone crime scene documented Lynagh's line of approach and flight from the scene and showed the significant areas adjacent to the victim's body, such as the haystack where Lynagh hid. Close-ups of Livingstone's multiple wounds and of an Oneida knife found beneath the haystack were all fragments of a much wider picture.

You cannot put a value on good observational skills, and such was the case when Sergeant Peter Holland spotted footprints. One might think that where Livingstone's body was discovered, on the sodden earth of the farm, heavily indented by the constant battering of calves' hooves, would not have been a good repository for minute evidence. In fact, it proved perfect for impression evidence. The muddy ground set a mould around anything pressed into it – such as the killer's shoe.

Following the killer's footprints led to the discovery of his escape route. Sergeant Peter Holland, attached to Monaghan Police Station, remarked: 'At the border-crossing point I saw fresh tracks made by either boots or shoes leading across the border into the South. It was pointed out to me by some member of the RUC who arrived on the scene that these footprints could be traced into the North, back to where the deceased's car had been abandoned'. Evidently, the killer had fled the scene, taken the victim's car and driven to a point just north of the border, abandoned the car and crossed the border into the south, perhaps thinking the law could not follow him there.

The detectives took plaster casts and a red wax lift from the footprint at the border crossing and at the farm. This provided a very distinctive impression of the left sole of a boot, consisting of broad ridges about the outside and eight short angular ridges along the centre. The sole had not been subjected to excessive wear.

But although James Lynagh was in custody, it didn't prove easy to retrieve his clothes and boots to compare against the footprints found at the scene. Sergeant Holland explained the problem:

'... When I entered the cell, I saw James Lynagh lying on the left-hand bunk bed. His feet were facing towards the cell door. I saw that he was wearing a pair of brownish red boots, which were wet and had mud and soil adhering to them. In addition, I saw there was a distinctive sole pattern on his boots and it remarkably resembled the footprints I had seen at Kiltybegs Border-Crossing point a short time earlier. I asked Lynagh to take off his shoes, that I wanted them for test purposes, and Lynagh refused. He replied to me that if I wanted his boots I would have to take them by force. I told him that he was obliged under the Criminal Law Act 1976 to hand over his boots for tests, but again Lynagh refused and said that if I wanted his boots I would have to take them by force ... Lynagh jumped up on the bunk bed and resisted as strenuously as he possibly could our efforts to remove his boots.'

Gardaí met similar resistance when they tried to take Lynagh's clothes, but it was vital to establish whether there had been a cross-transfer of substances from the scene to his clothes or vice versa. Sergeant Holland explained how Lynagh's clothes were eventually removed:

'Det Garda McCoy attempted to open the zip on the front of James Lynagh's jacket but he pushed Det Garda McCoy away. Garda Patrick McMorrow entered the room at this stage. D/Gda McCoy again asked James Lynagh to be sensible and remove his clothes and he replied, "Fuck off John, you will have to take them by force". Det Garda McCoy caught Lynagh's left arm as he started to resist. I then caught him [Lynagh] by the right arm and D/Gda McCoy caught his left arm. He [Lynagh] pulled back and came to rest against the table. He then began to kick with both feet. D/Gda Tadhg Foley and Gda Patrick McMorrow caught him by the legs. They began to remove his trousers. Lynagh continued to resist and kick and the table slipped and he fell to the floor. He continued to kick out viciously at D/Gda Foley and Garda McMorrow, but they succeeded in removing his trousers. D/Gda McCoy removed his jacket without much difficulty as Lynagh was concentrating in kicking D/Gda Foley and Gda McMorrow. He was also shouting at D/Gda Foley, he shouted, "You fucking Cork bastard," and at Garda McMorrow, "You red fucker, I'll get you yet".'

It was worth the struggle. I examined the soles of the boots and on the upper portions found considerable smearing of mud. The basic clay of the mud was the same as the clay adhering to the cast of the footprint at the border-crossing, and also the same as some of the samples of clay taken from the scene of the shooting. These differed markedly from control samples of sandy soil taken from Lynagh's home and other specified control areas. Adhering to the mud were pieces of hay, which also contained matching soil from the barn.

I compared the photographs of the footprints and they matched in size and pattern design. The footprint in the field beside the body was wet and muddy, but the ridge pattern was clearly visible and exactly the same as that on the soles of the boots of James Lynagh. The photo of the footprint found in the field beside the haystack was also of the same size and ridge pattern as the one found at the border.

Detectives also noticed that there was fresh clay on the bottom of Lynagh's trousers and shoes, which would be invaluable if it proved to be the same clay as that taken from the scene of the crime. Following examination, I found that the clay and grit from the trousers matched the clay and grit in the mud from the area adjacent to the barn at the scene of the shooting, and also matched samples taken at the border-crossing.

The method of comparison was to dry the soil at 105°C for two hours and then compare the colour. The samples taken from the Monaghan area, at the border, were much darker and greyer than the soil taken from the scene of the shooting. The clay at the scene of the shooting lacked humus and contained small white stones, small red stones and brittle black stones. The soil from the border-crossing differed from this. However, elements from both samples – silicon, potassium, calcium, titanium manganese and iron – were found on Lynagh's clothing.

The casts of the footprints taken at the border-crossing and the farm were an exact match with Lynagh's boots. By this is meant that the complicated ridge structure and the size were one and the same.

In the two side pockets and in a rear pocket of James Lynagh's trousers, I found a considerable number of pieces of hay, consisting of seeds, dried green grass and dried brown stalk material. Fragments of the hay matched others found in Livingstone's car, which had been used in the getaway.

Adhering to the rear thigh of the trousers were three pieces of binder twine. I analysed them on the comparison microscope, which allows two items to be viewed simultaneously. The pieces were the same colour as the binder twine from the barn, and matched in composition and bind of fibres.

On the front passenger seat of the getaway car I found five grey-blue cotton fibres, which were the same as some of the fibres used to manufacture the trousers James Lynagh had been wearing. The trousers were old and torn and wearing thin in a number of places.

Of the three suspects, only Lynagh refused to allow his hands to be swab-tested for the residue of firearms. 'You are no legal experts and you can quote that and section 52 to me, but I'll tell you it's only shit,' Sergeant Holland recorded him as saying. Instead, I took swabs from the pockets of his clothing, which can be legally seized, and it worked just as well. When a firearm is discharged, the explosion that expels the bullet gives rise to a cloud of gas, which emerges from the barrel of the gun and from around the firing mechanism. This gas carries dust containing metals: lead, copper, antimony and barium, which have been generated by the explosion within the barrel. The gun and any object in close proximity will be stained with traces of these four metals. Thus the residue on the hands and clothing of the gunman announce his guilt clearly. (It should be noted that it is also possible to pick up these metal traces by handling a recently discharged gun, even if one did not fire the gun.) Tests on Lynagh's clothing showed the presence of lead, copper, antimony and barium around the pockets, indicating that he had been in contact with a firearm.

James Lynagh was brought to trial for the murder of Henry Livingstone. The trial was conducted in the Special Criminal Court, Dublin. It was an important case legally: Lynagh was the first man to be tried in our jurisdiction for offences committed on the northern side of the border. Although the offence had taken place in Northern Ireland, Lynagh subsequently fled to the Republic. Under the Criminal Law Jurisdiction Act 1976, extradition was no longer required, and the border no longer afforded any protection to the criminal.

At the trial the judge deemed the forensic evidence to be 'strongly suspicious' in terms of linking Lynagh to the scene, but not enough to link him beyond reasonable doubt. Lynagh was acquitted of the murder and released without charge. His co-accused were also acquitted.

On 21 January 1981, James Lynagh struck again. This time the victim was eighty-six-year-old Sir Norman Stronge. It was an appallingly callous terrorist act. Sir Norman was a former Unionist MP and Speaker at Stormont Parliament. On the night of his assassination he was at his home, Tynan Abbey (near the border in Armagh), with his son, Jim, a retired member of the

Grenadier Guards and an RUC reservist. A group of men dressed in military-style uniform used explosives to blow their way through the front door. They ran through the house, sought out both men and executed them. They then firebombed the Stronges's ancestral mansion, reducing the beautiful building to rubble.

How could the death of an eighty-six-year-old man further their cause? A statement released by the Provisional IRA 'explained' that father and son had been put to death because they were 'unionist aristocrats'.

In November 1981, James Lynagh was again charged with membership of the IRA and again he was acquitted. By now he was also the prime suspect for the murder of William George Elliott from Charlemont in Armagh. Elliott was a former member of the UDR, a former executive of the Official Unionist Party and a former vice-chairman of the Central Armagh Unionist Association. He was murdered in the afternoon of Saturday, 28 June 1980 at a cattle market in Ballybay, County Monaghan. He was examining cattle in a pen when Lynagh walked up behind him, asked the man standing next to him to move aside, and shot Elliott four times in the head and back at point-blank range. The dead man's brother-in-law, Jack Donnelly, also a UDR man, was killed ten months later by the INLA.

George Elliott's widow took an action against the State through the European Commission on Human Rights. The Unionist Party's legal adviser, Edgar Graham, explained why: 'The constitution of the Republic is an encouragement to the IRA. The Dublin government claims jurisdiction over Northern Ireland and the IRA say they are trying to fulfil that claim. The aim of the unit in taking the case against the Dublin government is to ensure that their claim of jurisdiction is withdrawn and they take positive action on extradition.' In 1983 Edgar Graham was killed by the IRA.

Although James Lynagh never paid the judicial price for his crimes, it was probably just as well. If he had received a custodial sentence he would still be alive, probably free by now and no doubt back to his old tricks. As it turned out, his fate was more biblical: he lived by the sword and he died by it.

On 8 May 1987, Lynagh was shot dead by the SAS at Loughall, along with seven other members of the East Tyrone brigade of the IRA, and one unfortunate, innocent passerby, Anthony Hughes. The gang approached Loughgall RUC station a blue Toyota van, following a hijacked digger carrying a 200lb bomb. The RUC had received advance warning that an attack was likely. As the digger smashed through the gates of the station, with the bomb's fuse already lit, the SAS opened fire from several positions surrounding the van. The ferocity of the gunfire caused the van to burst into flames. A total of 1,200 bullets were fired. All of the dead had head wounds. Among the dead was James Lynagh.

The ambush of the gang was highly controversial – debate raged about an alleged 'shoot-to-kill' policy being operated by the SAS. Kevin McNamara, the Labour Party spokesman for Northern Ireland, condemned the shooting: 'I would much rather people were behind bars than under the ground. Behind bars they become the evil people they are and are arraigned before the civilised world for the type of plotting that they were doing.'

The RUC stated that the eight men had been intercepted while on a terrorist mission: the SAS acted to prevent their intended action of murdering RUC officers. Special Branch further stated that James Lynagh was a top assassin and an active terrorist who had been involved in several IRA operations in Tyrone in 1987. It was claimed he had been involved in an attack on the Birches RUC station near Portadown the previous year, carried out in exactly the same manner – with a digger and a van.

The RUC recovered the weapons carried by the IRA men killed at Loughall and concluded, on forensic examination, what was already known: they had been used in several killings of UDR men.

In May 2001 the Lynagh family was awarded £10,000 compensation for James's death. The European Court of Human Rights made the award on the basis that Lynagh's human rights had been violated by the actions of the SAS.

My connection with the Lynaghs extended beyond the Livingstone case. James's elder brother, Michael, committed suicide while in custody in Mountjoy Jail. He had been questioned in Rathmines Garda Station on 18 April 1982 in connection with the bombing of my car in January 1982. On 4 September 1982, while serving a sentence for another matter, he tied a sheet to the bars of his cell window and hanged himself.

CHAPTER 30: DEATH BY CHANCE
Deborah Robinson

A YOUNG NORTHERN IRISH WOMAN, Deborah Robinson, came to Dublin on 6 September 1980 on a blind date. The man she was due to meet was Edmund Law, son of Lord Ellenborough of England. Deborah met her date, but she never made it home. Her body was found two days later, on 8 September, in a ditch in County Kildare. She had been raped and strangled to death.

Deborah Robinson's last-known movements were described by Law, who said he had dropped her to the bus station. There the trail might have ended had her clothes not been sent to us for examination. Clinging to her garments was an unusual number of yarn fibres in a wide range of colours. The fibres must have come from a textile factory. Deborah was employed in such a factory, but this in itself did not provide a satisfactory explanation as it would not have been possible for the fibres to have stayed stuck to her clothes over such a long period of time. I concluded that the fibres had adhered shortly before her death.

The fibres provided gardaí with a lead: the variety of colours indicated that they had come from a small textile factory (larger factories work to big orders and are therefore unlikely to carry such a range). Detectives were put on the case and fibre samples were taken from every textile factory in Dublin City and County, and in counties Kildare and Meath. It was painstaking work, but eventually led to a match at a company called Janet Ltd. All of the male employees in the company were questioned.

The detectives quickly became very interested in the history of one employee in particular: Richard O'Hara. He was a twenty-eight-year-old Belfast man with criminal convictions for assault and theft, and he had quit his job on 10 September – four days after Deborah's murder. His letter of resignation outlined his plan to commit suicide.

A sample of O'Hara's blood was taken and was found to match the blood grouping found in the semen deposited in Deborah's body. Presented with this damning evidence, O'Hara made a full confession about the girl 'I killed on a Saturday in Dublin in September 1980.'

It was a classic and tragic case of being in the wrong place at the wrong time. Deborah Robinson and Richard O'Hara met by chance in the street and struck up a conversation – probably on the basis that they were both from Belfast. He told her he was driving to Belfast and offered her a lift – she probably trusted him on the basis that he had said he was married with three children. He then told her that he had to stop off in work on the way and they went to the textile factory. It was there that he raped and killed her, and there that the coloured fibres had attached to her clothing.

The chances of those two people meeting were as remote as the chances of gardaí ever linking O'Hara to the murder without forensic science.

CHAPTER 31: MASS DISASTERS

MY WORK CAN BE FULFILLING IN THAT I often have the satisfaction of knowing I have helped someone at a traumatic time in their life. Victims are the silent voices in our communities: people who go about their daily business and never cause any harm, but have the misfortune to be in the wrong place at the wrong time. Those times when I have been responsible for helping to put a criminal behind bars make everything I do worthwhile. However, I do have some regrets from my years fighting crime. I deeply regret the instances when forensic science could not help the victims, as was the case in two mass disasters. Unanswered questions linger over the Air India crash of 1985 in which over 300 people died, and the Stardust fire on St Valentine's Day 1981, in which forty-eight people were killed.

Air India Crash

On 22 June 1985, Air India flight 182 left Toronto, bound for Delhi, India, via Heathrow Airport, with a deadly cargo in the hold. Unbeknownst to captain, crew or passengers, a man had checked in his baggage at the airport, but he had never boarded the plane. He had good reason: his baggage contained a bomb timed to detonate while the plane was in the air.

The same man had also booked a ticket on flight 003 from Vancouver to Narita Airport in Japan. Again, the baggage made it on board, but the passenger did not.

At 7.13am (GMT) baggage-handlers were removing a suitcase from flight 003 at Narita when it exploded. Two baggage-handlers were killed and others injured. No one thought that the explosion might not be an isolated incident.

At 8.13am (GMT) flight 182 was approaching Heathrow after a trouble-free crossing. The captain radioed the tower to confirm that he was clear to land. Just moments later the plane exploded, at 31,000 feet, and crashed into the Atlantic Ocean off the south coast of Ireland. The nearest landfall was Ahakista, County Cork.

On 23 June, I travelled to Cork to attend the site of the disaster and collect evidence. I will never forget the scene that confronted me: a makeshift morgue of tents in a scene reminiscent of a battlefield. The recovery operation was led by the RAF. The rescue services pulled 132 bodies from the sea. The rest of bodies had not been recovered from the water, and never would be. The magnitude of the crime was overwhelming: a fellow human being had wilfully and deliberately set out to cause the deaths of over 300 innocent people.

We examined the recovered bodies in an attempt to isolate the cause of the explosion – at that point in time, a bombing was our best guess, but other possibilities had to be eliminated. From a forensic point of view, the fact that swathes of tissue lifted off the remains as easily as pages off a book was consistent with sudden decompression in a cabin, which causes the flesh to lift in flaps. Identification was straightforward as most of the faces and fingerprints were intact despite the fact that flesh was torn from the torsos and the thighs. Also, many of the passengers were Indian and, because of their cultural tradition of wearing jewellery, personal items being worn by the deceased could be readily identified by relatives.

Unfortunately, there were two bodies among those recovered that could not be identified. That was more the fault of the sea than the explosion, as bodies left any time in water will rot, get caught in rocks, or have their flesh nibbled away by shellfish. Such erosion makes identification very difficult, and sometimes impossible.

The Lab established from carbon monoxide levels in the victims' blood that there had been a fire on board before the crash, which lent credibility to the theory that the plane had been destroyed by a bomb. As the plane had taken off from Toronto it was deemed an act of terrorism against Canada, so the Canadian authorities were very much involved in every aspect of the investigation. They requested samples from the debris on which to perform tests, but could not reach a definitive conclusion as to the cause of the crash.

Since 1985 the Royal Canadian Mounted Police (RCMP) has been conducting the ongoing investigation. Experts worldwide have since concluded that the crash was indeed caused by a bomb, and the RCMP are working on that basis to find the people involved. One man, Inderjit Singh Reyat, has been convicted as a result of the investigation – he received a ten-year sentence in connection with the explosion at Narita Airport. Two other men, Ajaib Singh Bagri and Ripudaman Singh Malik, are due to go on trial in February 2002.

The Stardust Fire

The Stardust disaster was another of my personal regrets. The Stardust Ballroom was a totally unsuitable converted factory in Artane, Dublin, used for local discos. A St Valentine's night dance in 1981 ended in disaster when forty-eight young people died in a massive blaze that engulfed the building, and a further 214 were injured. The crowd was trapped inside the building because most of the fire doors were chained shut or otherwise obstructed. It was a devastating loss of so many young lives, and for relatives the pain has still not subsided.

The main purpose of the investigation was to establish if it had been started deliberately. The Irish government sent a forensics team to Birmingham to use the facilities they have for simulating the same fire conditions in exactly the same circumstances. These staged fires are filmed and tests conducted throughout. It proved impossible to conclude that the fire was anything other than an awful accident.

In the aftermath of the disaster, forty-three bodies were successfully identified and returned to their families for burial. However, we were unable to identify five bodies, and they have been buried together in a communal plot at Sutton cemetery, Dublin.

CHAPTER 32: THE DRUG BARONS

DRUGS HAVE LONG BEEN AND REMAIN the scourge of Western society. The presence of drugs leads to all kinds of law and order problems – problems that can decimate communities. The Forensic Science Laboratory took over drug analysis from the State Laboratory at the end of 1979, the year the Knocklong amphetamine factory was discovered by gardaí. The network of drug importation and drug-dealing had effectively been established from the late 1970s, but is was not to come into its own until the late 1980s. From 1983 to 1988 there was a hiatus, almost a cooling-off period, in which the gardaí dominated and it seemed that drug culture would not gain a significant foot-hold in Ireland. I was actually able to take scientists out of the drug analysis section, which has never happened since – it has always been the other way around.

The mid-1980s saw a sudden upsurge in drug importation and distribution. Drug addicts, or junkies as they are known, became a common sight in Dublin. These pathetic individuals were addicted to a Class A narcotic: diamorphine, or heroin. There were spates of robberies in hospitals and pharmacies as the addicts, desperate for heroin, attempted to pump any replacement, such as synthetic opiates and painkillers, into their bodies. Heroin changed the face of Dublin in the late 1980s, and the face of crime in Ireland. It was the age of the drug baron. In response, the drug analysis section of the Lab was organised into its own separate, distinct unit in 1985, and the gardaí stepped up their fight against the smugglers and dealers.

By 1988 heroin was being wrapped in plastic as against paper, which had been the norm in the early 1980s. The change came about so that users could carry their 'hit' around with them in their mouths, and swallow it if stopped by gardaí. The plastic protected the powder from enzymes and gastric juices and consequent degradation in the stomach, therefore it was still usable when passed out. It also meant that couriers, or 'stuffers', could carry it internally to thwart the efforts of customs officials to keep it out of the country. From a forensic scientist's point of view, this plastic wrapping opened up a whole new world of detection. Wrapping in itself can be very distinctive, enabling us to batch different consignments to their place of international origin. Plastic varies quite a lot, and during manufacture it will be pulled along rollers of varying strengths, so that if you look at it under polarised light you will see coloured striations that change with the run of the plastic. If you are lucky enough to get two separate ends of the same tear, you can find the striation running right through and link the packets.

Despite these advances in forensic detection, from 1988 drugs became an epidemic and simply mushroomed out of control. I think, to an extent, this was another area where the Northern 'Troubles' had a detrimental effect on people's sensibilities and sensitivities. I often felt that people took drugs to assuage the horrors of the times we were living in. But, of course, social economics was one of the biggest factors: it was no coincidence that the drug problem could be mapped demographically to areas of high unemployment and poor housing.

The popular drugs in the 1980s were mainly cannabis resin and, to a lesser extent, LSD (Lysergic acid diethylamide): it was as if Ireland realised it had missed the hippy age and was determined to catch up. But one of the most damaging drugs, heroin, was gradually consolidating its hold and changing the face of addiction as we knew it. In the 1990s, cocaine flooded the market and, as ecstasy would in the late 1990s, became the 'It' drug and elbowed out the likes of LSD. Like everything else in our consumerist society, drugs go through fashion trends. It was the task of the Gardaí and the Forensic Science Lab to be one step ahead of those trends.

During Ireland's presidency of the EU in 1996, the Lab proposed to undertake a project, under the auspices of the Department of Justice, to profile drug distribution across Europe. Slowly, Europol is putting the systems in place to exchange this information. It will be invaluable when it is put into full practice, but as Ireland tends to be at the end of the trail of supply, it is problematic to operate. However, the French have taken the concept very seriously. Their State Laboratory in Lyons receives a sample of every seizure of heroin over a kilogram, and draws up a profile, which is then compared and matched to other seizures nationally and internationally.

One area where forensics can give gardaí the edge in combating drugs is chemical profiling. No drug is a pure substance: most contain not only the basic drug, but many other components. In the case of heroin, it is mixed with diacetyle morphine, monacetyle morphine and five alkaloids (dangerous plant materials originating from the opium poppy). There are three chemicals used to transform morphine into heroin – acetic anhydride, acetic acid and hydrogen peroxide – and sugar is usually used to bulk it up. Other chemicals, like caffeine and paracetamol, will often be used as well. Pure heroin normally accounts for only 28–32 percent of the substance, although we have analysed batches containing up to 60 percent heroin, which is very pure not to mention lethal. Forensics can identify the presence or absence of these individual components and measure their quantity. This mix, or profile, enables various batches of drugs to be linked so that the supplier's route can be traced geographically – that is, if the consignments are found.

There are other ways to forensically trace batches of drugs. Sometimes you find fingerprints on the outside of the plastic packaging of dealers' quantities. Packages can also be linked to sources if they have been rubbed on the inside with menthol grease – a device intended to throw sniffer dogs off the scent, but which enables forensic comparison of the grease used. Drug-dealers also use carbon paper to absorb the odour of the chemicals used to convert morphine into heroin, but carbon paper also happens to be ideal for absorbing impressions, such as fingerprints.

However, even armed with these techniques we were contending with mafia-style drug barons willing to take incredible risks to cream off the drug wealth that was there for the taking. They policed each other with unprecedented brutality in order to maintain their lucrative lifestyles. In this bloody territorial war, the Dunnes were the first drug family.

There were sixteen offspring in the Dunne dynasty. The Dunne boys had been introduced to crime by their father, Christy Snr, who was convicted of manslaughter in 1939 and served his time in Portlaoise Jail, as his sons would thirty years later. Their mother was pregnant twenty-two times; sixteen of her children survived. The family lived in Vicar Street in the Liberties area of Dublin, and later moved to Rutland Avenue, Crumlin, not far from the Cahill boys.

The eldest of the boys was Christy Jnr, or Bronco, who had learned from a stint with Saor Éire how to go about pulling off an armed robbery and had then passed his skills on to his younger brothers: Shamie, Larry, Robert, Henry, Vianney, Mickey, Hubert (who drowned at the age of fourteen while residing at the Upton Reformatory School in Cork), Charlie (who showed Martin Cahill the ropes) and Gerard. The Dunnes were hitting jewellery stores before Cahill ever dreamed up the O'Connor heist, and doing so with a little more imagination, for example, Bronco dressed as a priest when they held up Breretons in Capel Street in 1976.

The Dunnes were the subject of police enquiries from an early age. On May 12, 1960, when he was just eight years old, Henry's face adorned the cover of the *Daily Mirror* under the headline: 'Anyone lost a son?' A police officer had noticed him stopping passersby on London Bridge asking them if they knew where his father was.

It was Larry who emerged as the Don Corleone figure. At twelve years of age he was before the courts for larceny and subsequently sent to the Industrial School in Letterfrack in Galway, then on to Daingean in Offaly (where Cahill was also dispatched). By now, Larry's elder brothers, Shamie and

Christy, were already hardened criminals specialising in theft of jewels. But it was Larry who realised the potential for drugs and set about establishing a network of supply. He became the country's first drugs baron. He coralled his brothers into the business and began making serious amounts of money.

In the circle of demand and supply, one person was essential to the success of the drugs barons: the stuffer or drugs courier. These people had high-risk, high-pay jobs, moving drugs through airports and facilitating international trade. Their cargo was usually carried internally, so as well as running the risk of being caught and imprisoned, they also ran the risk of drug packages bursting, which could cause serious internal damage or even death.

I recall one instance when one member of the notorious Dunne family – Shamie – was known to be about to import a consignment. Gardaí tracked him to the Burlington Hotel car park in Dublin, where he was arrested. Under the front passenger seat of his four-wheel drive, detectives found several kilos of cocaine wrapped in plastic. They searched a room in the hotel, which they suspected was being occupied by his contact, and in a bin in the bathroom found a package of cocaine wrapped in plastic and covered in sellotape. The room had just been vacated by a foreign woman who, by way of explanation, told gardaí that a man she didn't know had knocked at her door and asked to use her bathroom. She allowed him to do so. It was her contention that while he was in there he must have dumped the drugs in the bin. It was a good excuse as excuses go, because it left it to the gardaí to prove the pre-arranged deal between the pair.

The evidence arrived in the Lab for examination. The adhesive on the plastic packet found in the hotel bathroom matched that found under Shamie Dunne's passenger seat – but this in itself did not undermine the woman's story. However, the adhesive on both the bathroom and car packets had fibres matching the woman's clothing. She had three layers of garments and there were fibres from each layer present on the packets, significantly reducing the possibility of anyone else having deposited the trace evidence.

Stripmarks of glue had been found on her skin, under her chest, and these also came in for analysis. The glue from her body and the glue on the drug packets matched in composition. Physically, she was a very well-built woman with massively overhanging breasts and a small stomach, which enabled her, when using a judicious choice of clothing, to become one of the world's leading drug and currency smugglers – as her conviction sheet later revealed. She was duly prosecuted for the Burlington incident, but got off on appeal.

Despite Shamie's arrest, Larry was enjoying his heyday, indulging a personal penchant for handmade Italian shoes, Giorgio Armani suits, Lacoste shirts and flashy cars; at the time, about ten people died from drug-taking every year. Larry and his wife, Lily, removed themselves from Crumlin to a split-level mansion in Sandyford, overlooking the Dublin Mountains.

On October 12 1980 two garda units searched Larry's mansion. They found enough heroin in his home to make 5,283 deals. He had thirty-three previous convictions at the time. His trial began in the Central Criminal Court on 20 April 1983, with his henchmen in place to intimidate the members of the jury by staring deliberately at them. The jury was unable to reach a verdict against Larry and a retrial was ordered.

The second trial began on 22 June, and this time the jury had armed protection. Emotions were running high – drugs were wrecking whole communities and countless lives, and Larry Dunne was seen as the Grim Reaper, doling out death to make a quick buck. Garda hounds had to be brought in to keep anti-drugs demonstrators at bay; no other family had ever experienced such contempt from the public.

On the last day of his trial, Larry Dunne had lunch in the Molly Malone pub. He ordered soup and sandwiches and then used a pay call for a taxi. He had no intention of returning to court to receive his sentence. He dyed his hair red and made his way to Leitrim, from where he sailed down the River Shannon and waited until it was safe to travel to Le Havre in France. From there he moved to the Costa del Sol in Spain, where he worked as a shoe-shine boy, earning as much as £100 a day.

Years of testing heroin had given Larry a taste for it, but he had the funds to pay for a cure and flew to a detox clinic in Thailand. In 1985 he moved to Portugal, but was recognised by a policeman who was *au fait* with Interpol circulars. Extradited back to Ireland, he got fourteen years in 1985, but ten years later was released from Portlaoise. In March 1996, Larry and Lily buried one of their daughters who died from AIDS – the result of a lifelong drugs habit. But Larry had not learned anything from his loss or from his time inside. In May 1997 he was in court again, this time in Birmingham, charged with holding up a building society and attempted murder. He was convicted for the crimes.

It wasn't until December 1986 that the emerging Dunne matriarch, Larry's wife Lily, was also removed from the business. She received a nine-and-a-half-year sentence for dealing 374 packets of heroin. It seemed fitting that she should be sent down on the anniversary of her wedding to Larry, who at the time was serving his fourteen-year sentence in Limerick prison (he had been transferred there from Portlaoise). Before Lily Dunne was taken from court, her daughter Rachel and other family members took 'anniversary wishes' greeting cards from their bags and hurriedly signed them. Her daughters were aged eighteen, fifteen and eight. Her defence was that she was a hard-working person who had been sucked into drugs through her marriage. 'She has children who, if a custodial sentence is passed, will effectively be deprived of both parents. This is a heartbreaking situation for her as she still has a very young child of eight years,' her lawyer pleaded.

Practically the entire family, and some of those who married into it, was involved in drug-dealing. In jail, Larry was sharing a top-security wing with his brothers, Mickey and Henry. Mickey had received seven years for heroin dealing in 1982, and Henry got ten years in 1983 for possession of a firearm. Their elder brother, Christy Jnr, spent thirteen months in a Spanish prison for handling stolen cheques and being in possession of false passports, having previously faced drug charges in Dublin. The other brothers, Vianney, Francis and Gerard, also served time for possession of drugs. Mickey's wife, Dolores, got two years in 1982 on heroin charges, and Shamie's wife, Valerie, got three years for receiving stolen goods. A sister, Colette, did time for a drug-related offence, and another sister, Ellen, was charged with possession of heroin in 1982. Robert's wife, Theresa, faced similar charges at the same time.

Larry was back before the courts in January 2001 for beating a detective with a bamboo cane during a search at his nephew's house. Detectives attached to the National Drugs Unit were searching the house for cocaine. Larry's defence was that he did not know they were gardaí – despite the fact that they were wearing bibs emblazoned with the word 'Garda'. He claimed he thought they were members of Concerned Parents Against Drugs. He got three months.

The legacy of drug culture continues to infect Irish society. In 2000 'heroin illness' claimed lives in Dublin, Wicklow and Kildare. 'Heroin illness' is a euphemism for the deadly clostridium bacteria. In all, eight addicts died in Ireland and forty in England, Scotland and Wales. Death in each case was found to be caused by a bug found in a batch of heroin – a bug that is usually found in soil and animal droppings.

The drug scene in Dublin continues to make for depressing statistics. Currently, some 4,500 addicts are receiving methadone treatment, but over 8,000 have no contact with health board services. There are over 400 waiting to get places on heroin replacement programmes.

As a footnote to just how widespread the Dunnes's drug empire would become, it is interesting to note that in two decades inflation has not affected the price of 'gear'. In 1986, each of Lily's packets of heroin was valued at £10 in street value, which is roughly the same price today – an indication of just how over-supplied the market is.

The drug market continues to be a lucrative market, albeit an increasingly dangerous one for sellers. By 1984, the

Provisional IRA had gotten around to asserting dominance in the South by taking on anyone whose power-base threatened their own: namely, the drug barons. They asked Christy Dunne, Larry's brother, to supply a 'hit list' of the top twenty dealers in the South. Obviously, they wanted to know who was dealing and who they were dealing with. Christy Dunne gave them the list, and one of the prominent names was Martin Cahill, his old protégé. Every good student eventually leaves their teacher behind, but every good teacher keeps something in reserve. It would seem that Christy used the list as a chance to clear up some territories for himself. In 1994, Martin Cahill was gunned down in a Provo-style attack.

CHAPTER 33:
THE KILLING OF CAROL CARPENTER

ON 26 AUGUST 1988, SCHOOLGIRL Carol Carpenter left her home in Tallaght to go the local supermarket. Somewhere along the way she met her neighbour, Joseph Mark Dowling. He brought her into his house, attacked her and strangled her to death sometime between her disappearance on August 26 and the time when her body was found on August 28. Her battered body, with severe head and facial injuries, was dumped in bushes in the centre of Killinarden Park, about 100 yards from her home. This made our task a little more difficult as her body was found in a place other than where she had been killed.

Police investigations led to Dowling's house and made him prime suspect. The Lab carried out tests on blood stains found in his house. We could say, with a probability factor of a thousand million to one, that blood splashes found inside the house had come from Carol's body, giving gardaí their first definite lead. And we could also analyse the blood distribution. The particular pattern formation of blood stains on the fridge could only have been made if Carol had been lying down while she was being battered. Further tests proved that the blood in the house matched Carol's blood.

Dowling was arrested and a murder trial was scheduled. However, at the last minute he pleaded guilty to murder so no evidence was heard. A second charge of rape was not proceeded with.

CHAPTER 34: SADISTIC GAMES
Michael Bambrick

IN 1994, A NINE-YEAR-OLD GIRL WALKED into the garda station in Ronanstown, Dublin, and spoke to detectives about her father Michael. The detectives would later discover that her father was Ireland's answer to Jack the Ripper.

Adrienne Bambrick cried continuously as she told of being beaten for 'stealing bread' from the kitchen, of her father killing her pet dog and cat by slamming them against walls in front of her, and of the disappearance of her mother, Patricia McGauley.

Gardaí had always suspected that Michael Bambrick was involved in the disappearance of his common-law wife in 1991, but they had been unable to establish any leads. They knew the couple had had a violent row before Patricia vanished from their home at 57 St Ronan's Park, because neighbours reported hearing a woman's screams that evening, lasting for a period of two hours; the sound would have been much louder from Adrienne's bedroom. However, a number of witnesses had also reported seeing a woman they presumed to be Patricia –

dressed in her clothes – storm out of the house that evening. Michael Bambrick's story that she had left him could not be undermined.

Michael Bambrick and Patricia McGauley were both recovering from broken marriages when they met in 1982, but by the time of Patricia's disappearance in 1991 they had been together for nine years and had two children: Adrienne (nine) and Louise (seven). Bambrick's first wife had left him in 1974, not because she had just discovered her husband was a transvestite but because he had almost killed her while indulging his taste for sado-masochistic bondage. After they split up, he indecently assaulted one of her friends, threatening to kill her and her child if she told the gardaí. Nonetheless, the women went ahead and pressed charges. He was convicted and received a six-year suspended sentence. A pattern for extreme violence was well established by the time he hooked up with Patricia.

On 11 September 1991, Bambrick finally acted out in full the fantasies he had inflicted on his wife and her friend He tied Patricia's hands behind her back with a pair of tights, put a second pair in her mouth and choked her until she was dead. The following morning he took the two children to school, went to his FÁS course job and collected Patricia's social welfare money.

The next day, he dismembered Patricia in the boxroom. He removed her breasts – an action common to many sex murderers. He piled her remains into plastic bags, which he threw over the garden wall onto a footpath on the other side. He then jumped over the wall, transported the bag with its terrible cargo on his bike to Balgaddy dump about a mile away and covered what was left of Patricia with clay.

Michael went to the Bridewell Garda Station and reported Patricia as a missing person. He adopted the role of a concerned partner by going around their old haunts asking if anyone had seen her. He displayed no guilt and no remorse, just the caring anxiety of a worried partner.

When Patricia's relatives visited the house to see how the girls were doing in their mother's absence, they were struck by how unusually clean the house was. But gardaí could not search a house on the basis that they believed a murder might have taken place. And, of course, neighbours claimed to have seen Patricia leaving the house, of her own accord, on the night she disappeared.

There the trail went cold – until Bambrick's desire to gratify himself re-emerged. In 1992 he met a single mother, Mary Cummins, in a pub. They were seen drinking and chatting by several witnesses before they left the pub, together. They went first to Mary's house to put away her shopping and then went on to Bambrick's house. Unsuspecting Mary Cummins would meet the same fate as Patricia.

Here again, Bambrick's little girl was watching everything, taking it all in. Mingled with Adrienne's stories of abuse the day she arrived in Ronanstown Garda Station was the story of a woman she met in the pub with her father, and of the woman's little girl with whom she had played. She told how she had gone with her father to the woman's house and helped her put away her shopping. She told how the woman was kind to her and had given her a present of a Coca Cola flask. She told how the woman had got a taxi with her and her father back to their home in St Ronan's Park. When Adrienne woke up the next morning the woman was gone, but she had left behind her clothes and shoes, which her father then burned, she said.

These little clues turned out to be of great importance. Gardaí were able to corroborate her story because Mary Cummins's nephew confirmed that he had given his aunt several limited edition, promotional Coca Cola flasks just days earlier. The gardaí did not have a body, but the flask was enough to put Michael Bambrick in the company of Mary Cummins on the night she disappeared.

Fearing the worst for the two women, the investigating gardaí next got in touch with the Gloucester police in England – the force who had trawled Fred West's garden and made such gruesome findings. On their advice the gardaí put a mechanical digger into Bambrick's back garden and began searching. The Lucan team were hoping to avoid publicity, but it was impossible to hide the presence of a digger at the house. They found bones in the garden, but they belonged to a dog. They also discovered blood on a mattress of an upstairs bedroom, but Bambrick claimed it had been soiled when Patricia had had a miscarriage.

On 19 May 1994, our team of forensic scientists began a three-day examination of the interior of the house, looking for the presence of blood on furniture, floors and fittings. Although blood stains may be cleaned up and made invisible to the naked eye, they are very difficult to remove completely and can be detected with chemicals. In Bambrick's house we got fifty positive reactions – indicating the presence of blood. There was so much, in fact, that blood had even seeped right through the floorboards.

On the strength of this, Bambrick was arrested and taken in for questioning. His latest girlfriend, who was pregnant by him, told gardaí that he had admitted to her that he had once killed a girl. There were also claims that he was interfering with children. It was imperative that he be put away, so everything hinged on the evidence. However, half an hour into his interrogation, Bambrick unexpectedly admitted his crimes. He said he had killed and dismembered Patricia McGauley and Mary Cummins, and agreed to bring gardaí to the burial site – Balgaddy dump. He also confessed that he had previously returned to the scene of his crime to check that his tracks were covered. He had discovered a head sticking out in the open from beneath the debris of the dump, and had dropped a concrete block on it to destroy it.

The gardaí weren't too hopeful of uncovering suitable evidence, as anything that might be found would undoubtedly be in a serious state of decay. Furthermore, much of the rubbish and soil had been transferred to Finglas. The gardaí began sifting through the rotting materials and very soon found fragments of skull, tibia and thigh – many with jagged marks consistent with the edge of a saw.

On 26 July 1996, Michael Bambrick was sentenced to eighteen years' imprisonment for the manslaughter of his two victims. He was not convicted of murder because the act was not deemed to be premeditated. The court ruled accidental death, based on the acceptance that it was, in fact, a botched sex game rather than a deliberate attempt to kill.

CHAPTER 35: MAD OR BAD?
The Trial of Brendan O'Donnell

ABSOLUTE EVIL IS EXPLOITED IN TIMES OF WAR, but is relatively rare in times of peace. One of those rare times was 1994. Evil shows its face when inexplicably random acts of violence are perpetrated against the innocent. The lack of reason or motive adds a chilling dimension to any murder. Such mindlessness is impossible to fathom. When a man or woman murders deliberately and simply for murder's sake, they step beyond the bounds of human experience and understanding. They become feared and loathed in equal measure.

In the case of triple-murderer Brendan O'Donnell, most people found it easier to create reasons than accept there were none. The impetus for his crimes was traced back to his childhood. It was alleged that he was physically abused by his father. His mother had committed suicide when he was a boy, and he apparently had slept on her grave for comfort, fending for himself and living in a shed until taken in by a neighbour. Many commentators argued that O'Donnell had exacted his revenge as an adult, choosing as his victims a mother and child to replicate the circumstances of his own loss – but this time casting himself in the role of the one in control. However, the fact that one of his victims, Imelda Riney, had been raped before she was murdered does not fit this picture.

O'Donnell's week of murder began on 29 April 1994. He abducted Imelda Riney and her three-year-old son, Liam, from their remote home in Whitehead, County Clare. He forced Imelda to drive to Cregg Woods. There he shot Imelda, then brought Liam over beside the body of his mother and shot him in the head.

Sometime between 3 and 4 May, O'Donnell approached Fr Joseph Walsh of Eyrecourt, County Galway, possibly to confess. No one is sure what transpired between the men, but it is known that they drove to Cregg Woods – back to the scene of the crime. O'Donnell made Fr Walsh kneel down on the ground and he held a gun to his head. Again, we will never know what exactly happened, but the indentations in the ground suggest that the priest was kneeling for quite some time. It is likely he attempted to reason with O'Donnell and to beg for his life. Unfortunately, O'Donnell could not be reasoned with. He shot Fr Walsh dead.

On 6 May Fr Walsh's car was found burnt out by the shores of Lough Derg. By now, Imelda and Liam had also been reported missing and gardaí were very anxious to get some answers. Then, O'Donnell struck again. On the night of 7 May he broke into the Sampson home in Whitehead. He ordered eighteen-year-old Fiona Sampson from her bed. At gunpoint, he walked Fiona some three or four miles – barefoot and in her nightclothes – across a bog. When O'Donnell spotted a car approaching on the road, he forced the driver to stop and ordered Fiona into the backseat. He too sat into the back of the car and, holding his .22 rifle to the back of the driver's head, he ordered him to drive. The driver was a seventy-four-year-old retired farmer, Edward Cleary, who later admitted that he was sure O'Donnell was going to shoot him.

When Fiona's family reported her missing, the gardaí quickly made a connection between the various unexplained events. They put a security cordon around the area and began checking all cars. Their quick action prevented more deaths. The car containing the three was stopped. Two officers, Detectives James Breen and Pat O'Donnell, disarmed O'Donnell and pulled Fiona Sampson and Edward Cleary to safety.

Between 7 and 8 May, gardaí discovered the bodies of O'Donnell's victims. Fr Walsh was found lying on the gound in Cregg Woods, while Imelda and little Liam were found in a shallow grave about 150 yards from the priest.

At the outset of the investigation, the main plank of the State's evidence against O'Donnell was the testimony of his last victim, Fiona Sampson, who had lived to tell the tale of her abduction by him and his threats to rape and kill her. Gardaí located the murder weapon, but there was difficulty matching the bullets in that O'Donnell had used .22 bullets and had fired them through the back of the neck of the priest and young mother at point-blank range. The bullets had distorted as they went through bone and could not be linked back to the weapon. Therefore, to make the case watertight, we needed the fibres and hairs and blood which must have been exchanged during his contact with those he had killed. It meant that a forensic examination of O'Donnell's clothing was crucial.

When O'Donnell refused to hand over his clothes, gardaí quoted the section of law that gave them the right to take them, to which he replied, 'I know about forensic science' – hardly the words of the profoundly deranged! Nevertheless, his clothes were removed and delivered to the Lab. We found three fibres on his garments matching Imelda Riney's clothing. O'Donnell was also asked for a blood sample, which we needed to connect him to the semen found in Imelda Riney's body. In this, legally, O'Donnell did have a choice and could refuse. He asked why the sample was required and gardaí told him that if he were innocent, it would rule him out of their enquiries. He refused, as those with guilty consciences often do. As it happened, it didn't matter. On his underpants we discovered a tiny quantity of semen, enough to match his DNA with that of the semen found in Imelda Riney's body. It could only have been generated by him.

The trail of forensic evidence did not end there. Although O'Donnell had worn gloves to avoid leaving fingerprints, he had broken a window when entering the priest's house. On his gloves we found fragments of glass, which matched in refractive index and composition the shattered pane from the house.

The trial of Brendan O'Donnell was to become the lengthiest in the State up to that time. In Whitegate, County Clare, at the age of twenty-one, O'Donnell had returned to the place of his upbringing and put a single-barrelled rifle up to a three-year-old's eye and fired because, we were led to believe in court, he was 'mad' not 'bad'. So went the essence of his defence. However, the guilty but insane plea relies on the insane not being held responsible for their actions, that is, it must be proven that they were unaware that what they were doing was wrong. The fact that, while in custody, O'Donnell had had the presence of mind to refuse to hand over for forensic examination the clothes he had been wearing when he carried out the executions was not considered admissible in a court of law.

As the 'mad or bad' argument raged, it was clear even the psychiatrists were divided in opinion. He was sane, a sociopath, or a schizophrenic, depending on whom you believed. 'Badness' was the verdict of Dr Art O'Connor, consultant psychiatrist at the Central Mental Hospital in Dundrum. Under cross-examination, O'Donnell told how he had taken his instructions from the devil, which was a little too clichéd for my liking. When asked if the devil was in court, he pointed to the press bench! When asked why he had killed Imelda Riney, he said the devil had told him to.

O'Donnell's defence team lodged a plea of guilty but insane. Experts debated the definition of insanity – a legal rather than psychological concept. Many defendants see the plea as an 'easy' option: it is always preferable to end up incarcerated in the Central Mental Hospital rather than in Mountjoy Jail because, as demonstrated by the case of double-murderer John Gallagher, the insane have enormous rights.

In O'Donnell's case, the jury was unwilling to let him off the hook. The jury did not believe his tales of giant butterflies buzzing around him in his cell, nor his accounts of being attacked by a giant pheasant, of a woman turning into a cat and of a voice telling him to call all the prison-warders 'Seamus'. In April 1996, O'Donnell was found guilty of murder in all three instances. He received three consecutive life sentences, to be served at Mountjoy Jail.

He was transferred to the prison, but his behaviour was disruptive, unpredictable and hard to supervise twenty-four hours a day. He was transferred to the Central Mental Hospital for a spell in 1997. He died there due to an adverse reaction to his medication. The coroner at his inquest returned a verdict of 'death by misadventure'.

Some say only a madman could have done what he did. But the truth is every man is capable of evil and every man makes his own choices in life. Evil and insanity do not have to be bedfellows, the sanest men can commit the worst brutalities.

The guilty but insane plea has proven controversial in murder trials. For the criminals, there are good reasons to plead insanity: those found guilty but insane are remanded to the Central Mental Hospital, usually for an indeterminate period, whereas those found guilty are give a mandatory life sentence in prison; if the criminally insane abscond from the State, the government has no power to extradite them back home; the insane have the right to be released when they are deemed well again – unlike murderers who are only ever released back into society on 'license' from their life sentence and at the ultimate discretion of the Department of Justice (Although life usually means around ten years for the guilty and sane, some release licenses would amount to political suicide for a government and are repeatedly 'long fingered', as seen in the case of lifers like John Shaw, Geoffrey Evans and Malcolm McArthur. But if these men had been declared insane, their cases would be reviewed under different criteria.)

The current law governing criminal insanity dates to 1883, and many commentators argue that it is simply too dated to deal with twenty-first century crime. The loopholes in the

Criminal Lunatics Act 1883 became glaringly apparent in the case of double-murderer John Gallagher. In 1988 Gallagher was charged with being guilty, but insane, of the murder of Ann Gillespie (18) and her mother, Annie in the grounds of Sligo General Hospital. He was remanded to the Central Mental Hospital. He escaped from the hospital in 2000 and went on the run to England. British police later arrested Gallagher, under Britain's Mental Health Act, in a supermarket car park in Oxford, but under current Irish law he cannot be extradited back to this country.

The seriousness of the Gallagher case has led the government to draft a new proposal: the Criminal Law (Insanity) Bill 2001. This should address some key points, but has yet to be ratified and put into practice.

For my part, I would like to see the introduction of an alternative plea to 'Guilty but Insane', given the frequency with which dangerous criminals now resort to that plea. Other countries have recourse to the plea of 'Diminished Responsibility', which means 'out of one's mind at the time the act was committed', and, if accepted, ensures that the defendant receives a sentence of manslaughter rather than murder. If it were applicable in Irish courts, it would widen the gap between the sane and the insane, making the latter harder to prove, therefore criminals could not take advantage of the 'Guilty but Insane' plea so easily.

CHAPTER 36: DEATH BY CRUCIFIXION

PAUD SKEHAN, A SIXTY-EIGHT-YEAR-OLD MAN living in Bridge-town, County Clare, was beaten up during a robbery of his home some time between April 9 and 19 1998. The beating was vicious, but the torture was far from over. While he was still alive, Paud Skehan was blindfolded, his hands and feet were tied with television cable wire, he was suspended out over a banister rail in an inverted crucifixion position and doused with petrol.

It was an awful, awful death. Paud was left there for a number of hours in terrible pain until he slipped into unconsciousness. He was later discovered by a neighbour who heard him moaning in pain. The battered pensioner was rescued and brought to hospital, but he never came out of the coma – a typical outcome of a crucifixion death as it causes pooling of blood in the brain, heart and lungs. He died on 3 June from his extensive injuries.

Gardaí were obviously very anxious to catch the person capable of such random and brutal violence. They delivered the floorboards from the dead man's home to the Lab, and Dr Thomas Hannigan treated the blood with a chemical process known as amido black, designed to enhance marks made in blood and show the finer detail. It was clear from the blood-spatter distribution that the victim had been dripping blood onto the floor below rather than spurting it, indicating that he had been beaten by the killer *before* being suspended. This implied deliberateness in the crime and thus meant the crucial difference between a murder and a manslaughter charge.

A large section of the blood staining showed a 'dragging formation', indicating that he had been beaten in one area of the house and then dragged across the floor to the banisters. More importantly, in the dragging stain we found footprints made by a Fila runner. While more than 100,000 Fila runners are imported into the country, on average, each year, the brand comes with different styles, sole patterns and sizes. The footprint matched the sole of the shoe of prime suspect Willie Campion (a local, known criminal), but he was denying any involvement. In fact he was 'putting it up' to the Lab, remarking that is was 'up to your scientists to prove it'. Campion also claimed that forensic evidence 'proves the runners were there. It doesn't prove I was there.'

Campion failed to take into account the fact that a footprint is very distinctive. It wouldn't matter if everybody were wearing the same pattern on the sole of their shoe because each individual's way of walking will create a new pattern. Some people walk on their toes, some in the centre, some wear down the heels. It's very distinctive.

The substance that shoe soles are made of is Polymer, which is like putty. This means they will pick up little bits of metal or sharp stones or glass, which again leaves individual indentations. The odds against exact matches between two shoeprints are astronomical; as evidence, it's conclusive.

When gardaí informed Campion of this aspect of forensic evidence, he said 'runners can't talk and the man is dead.' But, of course, he was wrong. Campion got life.

CHAPTER 37: MURDER IN CARRAROE
The Lonely Death of Siobhán Hynes

ON DECEMBER 6 1998 A HORRIFIC CRIME took place at a quiet, beautiful beach on the west coast of Ireland. The murder of seventeen-year-old Siobhán Hynes caused outrage and revulsion nationwide. The number of crimes against women has been steadily increasing over the last five years, but the rape and murder of Siobhán reached a new low of depravity. The entire country wanted to see the perpetrator caught and imprisoned.

John McDonagh was charged with the rape and murder. He was a local man, a twenty-seven-year-old builder's labourer. It was alleged that he had worked himself into a rage after an argument with his ex-girlfriend, and was out for revenge when he happened upon Siobhán. She was out with friends, but had decided to go home early and not attend the local disco with the others.

The jury heard how Siobhán was taken to Tishmean beach in Carraroe and there raped with an object. Her killer attempted to strangle her, and then left her for dead in a rocky inlet, obviously hoping that she would be dragged out by the tide and never found. The post-mortem examination would later conclude that Siobhán died as a result of drowning and compression of the neck.

In June 2001, John McDonagh came before the Central Criminal Court charged with the crime. The conviction depended on the forensic evidence and the jury's understanding of the significance of our findings. There was a lot of evidence and the expert witnesses had to talk the jury through every item.

The jury was sent out to deliberate. On two occasions the foreman of the jury requested that the nature of the scientific evidence against the accused be further explained. Mr Justice Pat Smith read back over the entire transcript of the testimony given by Dr Louise McKenna, a forensic scientist attached to the Lab.

The jury was reminded that Dr McKenna had found 'numerous' fibres that matched the dead girl's acrylic, wine polo-neck, her blue polyester fleece jacket and her black socks on a jumper worn by John McDonagh. Dr McKenna had also found two red fibres, which matched McDonagh's car seat cover, on Siobhán Hynes's clothes. The possibility of the fibres originating from three sources other than the girl's clothing was 'very remote'. The cross-transfer of fibres lent 'very strong support that (the schoolgirl) was in contact with (the accused's) jumper and strong support for her being in his car.' Dr McKenna chose the words 'very strong' and 'strong' from a six-point scale used in such analysis, which ranges from no support, slight support, support, strong support, to very strong support.

The defence counsel, Mr Barry White SC, argued that 'numerous' was a 'rather unscientific description', but Dr McKenna explained that it is the standard term used when more than fifteen matches are found. In fact, she had found twenty-five fibres that matched the fleece and twenty that matched the polo-neck, and at that point she stopped looking. Some laboratories stop looking after matching six fibres.

Mr White's case was that Dr McKenna's evidence was 'one of the linchpins of the State's case, but all that Dr McKenna can say is that those fibres matched the schoolgirl's clothes.' The scientist could not say that they were definitely from those particular clothes, he said. It seemed that forensic science itself was in the dock: the defence counsel was questioning the validity of Dr McKenna's conclusion.

However, if the jury were in any way swayed by this argument, the report of McDonagh's behaviour after the incident had the opposite effect. When gardaí asked him to hand over the clothing he had been wearing on 6 December for fibre analysis, he handed over the wrong clothing. Gardai discovered what he was up to when they examined closed circuit TV evidence from the night in question, and realised he had not handed over the jumper he had been wearing. McDonagh's excuse was that they had asked him for 'a jumper', not '*the* jumper'.

Gardaí informed him of the results of the forensic tests which had matched fibres from Siobhán's clothes to fibres found on his jumper. McDonagh replied that most people in Galway had a maroon jumper of some sort since it was the county colour. When they asked him how fibres from his black-and-red car seat cover could have ended up on Siobhán's clothing, he said that most people in Carraroe had a black-and-red seat cover as those were the Carraroe colours.

During his interrogation, gardaí had pressed him further on this: 'Can you explain why fibres from Siobhán Hynes's fleece and jumper were found on your jumper? ... Tell us the truth. For the sake of your family ... Forensic scientists can link Siobhán Hynes to your clothes and to your car?' His reply was the closest they would get to an admission: 'I know I can't dispute what the scientist says.'

On 17 June 2001, the jury found John McDonagh guilty of murder and of Section 4 rape, that is, rape with an object causing severe mutilation. McDonagh was sentenced to life for Siobhán's murder and received a ten-year sentence for the rape, to be served concurrently.

EPILOGUE:
THE FUTURE OF FORENSICS
IN IRELAND

JUST AS MARTIN CAHILL HAD TRIED TO DESTROY ME in 1982, in 1992 the IRA attempted to destroy the Forensic Science Lab in Northern Ireland with a bomb, devastating the building and its contents – at least temporarily. As with Cahill's destructive act, this showed the fear of forensics in the criminal community. Through science we *can* beat them and we *can* help ourselves, and this is what the criminals wish to destroy.

However, science is not so fragile. The Northern Ireland Lab continues to thrive, as does the southern Lab, still based in the Phoenix Park. Ironically, the park has been the scene of considerable criminal activity over the years. It was here Malcolm McArthur murdered Bridie Gargan; a German tourist was mugged and killed in his tent; and heroin addicts continue to overdose regularly within the quiet precincts of the park. You might say that the Phoenix Park is a microcosm of the shift in Irish society over the last decade: like a Petri dish containing a sample of the crime culture.

My own role as Director of the Laboratory is changing. There has been a much greater emphasis on administration. The government's policies on strategic management, business plans, performance management, development systems and partnerships have seen to that. It is a long time since I played a hands-on role in so far as the science is involved. One of my weekly tasks, and one that I see as essential, is showing garda recruits around the Lab. This is of vital importance in their training, as future gardaí are the hope on which we depend. It is also very necessary to keep in contact with the Lab's customers.

In recent years I have travelled abroad quite a lot to attend international conferences as the forensic science community becomes more of a family in which rules and regulations are laid down internationally. There are regular conventions in Britain to discuss the position of forensic science in Britain and Ireland. Europe, too, takes the subject very seriously. EU framework directives regularly award funds for research, generally to projects involving cooperation between member states.

In the late 1990s I was invited to speak in Israel and Poland. The Lab is a member of the International Association of Forensic Sciences, which meets every three years. The last three meetings were held in Dusseldorf, Tokyo and Los Angeles, respectively. The next, in 2002, will be held in France. The Lab was also one of the founding members of the European Network of Forensic Science Institutes in 1992, and this organisation has spread to include most European countries. We have hosted two major conferences, one in 1996 and the last in 2000, which was attended by 377 forensic scientists from twenty-six countries. The occasion marked the celebration of the twenty-fifth anniversary of the Lab.

The Lab has enjoyed considerable success over the yea.
and we have formed a close and fruitful partnership with the
gardaí. The job of the gardaí is becoming more and more difficult as crime becomes more sophisticated and criminals
become more violent. The Garda Siochána is in the front line –
forensics provides the back-up.

Our work – that of the gardaí and the Lab – would greatly
benefit from the adoption of a DNA database, that is, if the
gardaí were given the power, like other police forces around
the world, to take mouth swabs for DNA controls. Currently,
samples from a suspect can be retained here for only six months
after the crime. But if we could keep them indefinitely, culprits
who re-offend and leave some of their blood, semen or other
body fluids at the scene could be 'matched' or 'hit' quickly.

The most developed system is in Britain, where they have
two different kinds of database: a criminal intelligence database and a database of unsolved crimes. The former holds the
profiles of over 300,000 persons convicted, charged or suspected of criminal activity, the latter holds the profiles of stain
samples from approximately 30,000 unsolved crimes. By the
start of 1999, 17,000 people had been linked to crimes via the
database and 4,500 crimes were linked to similar crimes. The
Forensic Science Laboratory in Northern Ireland has also started
to establish a database and has recorded hundreds of hits for
crimes, including sexual assault In one case, the rapist's DNA
profile was identified from saliva on chewing gum left in the victim's hair. He was on the database for car stealing. In another
case, the DNA of a man convicted of handling stolen goods was
matched to that of semen found in cases of sexual assault on
prostitutes.

The legislation for databases in Britain is based on that which governs fingerprints. Other European countries either have or are in the process of drafting legislation for DNA databases. Some governments have opted to appease civil rights groups by agreeing to create databases only on criminals convicted for crimes with a minimum sentence of three years' imprisonment. Currently there are no proposals for a national database in Ireland.

*   *   *

In wet weather, when my limbs ache and amplify old injuries, I sometimes think: what if I had stayed in Erin Foods – the first company I worked for whilst researching my PhD. But then, I can't see myself ever having been satisfied sipping soup.